Table of Contents

Hog Hunting Success is Found Right Here in this Book

In this book I teach you all of the essentials to achieve the best results possible in the sport of hog hunting. It is my goal to save you the pain, heartache and lost time that many hunters experience when hunting hog.

Attention All Hog Hunters...

This Is A Step-By-Step Guide To Hog Hunting With No Step Missed

Easy to Understand Illustrations

In the book I provide several easy to understand illustrations to help you with the basic concepts of hog hunting. These will help you quickly visualize the concepts explained in the book to be sure you understand each tactic. Below is one example.

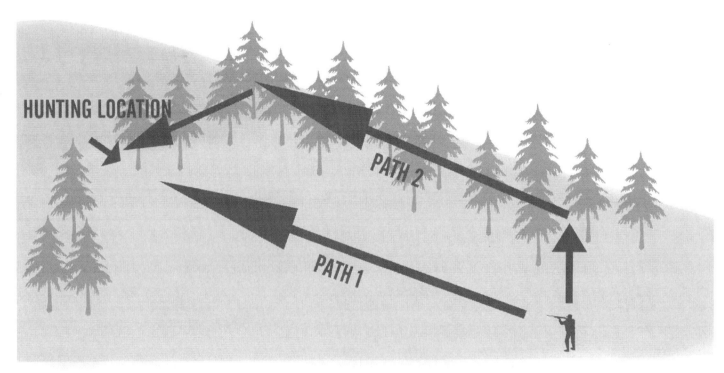

WALKING TO YOUR HUNTING SPOT

HUNTING LOCATION

PATH 2

PATH 1

WIND DIRECTION

Common Mistakes Made by Hog Hunters:

1. Not using the wind and sun to their advantage

2. Hunting in the wrong locations

3. Using poor shooting techniques

How Do You Avoid These Mistakes?

In this book I will equip you with the knowledge you need to immediately experience success with hog hunting. Put these lessons into action to avoid or discontinue making the common mistakes.

Who Can Benefit from This Book?

I provide relevant information for people with the following experience levels:

- People curious about hog hunting

- People ready to start hog hunting

- Novice hog hunters

- Hog hunters struggling for success

Now let's get started...

Step 1: Why Hunt Hogs?

Hog Hunting Makes for Fun Experiences

As we get started, it is important to understand why you would want to hunt hogs. There are several reasons to consider hunting hogs including its challenges, multiple hunting methods and skills that translate to hunting other game. In this section, I will cover the most common reasons people hunt hogs and get you thinking if hog hunting is a sport that is right for you.

Reasons to Hunt Hogs:

- Experience new locations
- Relaxing
- Practice for other hunting
- Great exercise
- Challenging
- Taste great & fills the freezer
- Trophy Opportunities

Experience New Locations

Hog hunting is often done in remote places. Unless you live near prime hog hunting land, you will need to travel to go hog hunting which allows you to experience these new locations. Even if you are hunting in a place that is not all that far away, it will likely be a place that you do not go to on a regular basis. If you are a person interested in hog hunting you are probably interested in the outdoors, so a chance to see some new outdoor terrain will likely appeal to you.

Relaxing

Although hog hunting can require a lot of work, it can also be quite relaxing. This sport forces you to get into the outdoors and experience the wilderness with minimal if any connection to the outside world. With today's face paced and connected lifestyles many people find that hog hunting can help them refocus and relax while they are on their hunting trip.

Great Practice for Other Hunting

One great benefit of hog hunting is that it is an excellent way to learn and teach hunting skills. I am not saying that hog hunting is easy, but it does provide for good learning opportunities. For beginning hunters, the skills you can learn with hog hunting are transferable to other types of hunting, especially big game hunting. The skills include shooting moving game, proper concealment, decoying and stalking. This means that you can use the trial and error that happens during hog hunting other elusive species.

Great Exercise

Hog hunting is a sport that can provide incredible exercise. For example, if you plan on hunting hogs with the stalking method, you are going to be in for quite a workout. A single day of stalking hogs could include be many miles of walking in an effort to find your game. Often this will include going through some challenging terrain such as tall hills, valleys and thick woods and vegetation. All of these situations will certainly challenge you physically. Before you head out hog hunting, you should put this physical component into consideration. It is best to spend some time in advance getting your fitness up to a level that can withstand these conditions, so you are not left physically exhausted in the middle of your hunt.

Challenging

Once you begin hunting hogs, you will realize that this can be a challenging sport but its challenges can make for great enjoyment. To be successful with hog hunting you need to understand hog behavior, concealment, decoying and proper shooting techniques. Unlike some game hunting such as squirrel, dove and waterfowl hunting, the success rates are sometimes be lower each time you get out hunting. However, this makes the sport fun because it is not a sport that you typically just happen upon having success. So when you are successful, it is satisfying because you were able to fool these elusive animals.

Taste Great

Another reason is that hogs can have a great flavor. Unlike some game animals such as squirrels, chipmunks, geese, and even ducks a lot of people find the flavor of hogs to be quite tasty. So with hog hunting not only can this be a fun outdoors activity but it can also produce some very tasty and unique meals that you could share with friends and family. It can be a great conversation piece when you prepare hogs for visitors.

Trophy Opportunities

If you are looking for a big game trophy that you can be proud to display for years then hog hunting is perfect for you. A boar mount is an impressive specimen that you can proudly display for others to admire as they come to your home. Adding a boar mount to your existing game display will undoubtedly turn some heads!

What Hog Hunting is Not

- **CHEAP:** There are all sorts of costs including equipment, travel, license, food, meat processing and taxidermy to name a few.
- **EASY:** Although the sport can be relaxing it is not easy. For successful hog hunting, it will require plenty of physical activity.
- **QUICK:** The most successful hog hunters will invest hours in planning their hunts, studying maps and hours in the field finding hogs.
- **WITHOUT RISK:** Sure there are a lot of things you can do to make hog hunting safer. However, there are plenty of risks with the sport including hogs charging at humans, inclement weather and wilderness survival.

Now let's examine weapons to use for hog hunting...

Step 2: Weapons for Shooting Hogs

Select from a Variety of Guns for Hunting Hogs

A great aspect that keeps hog hunting interesting is the wide range of weapons you can choose from to hunt these animals. Each type of weapon has its own unique strengths and challenges for hunting hogs. To mix up your hog hunting you can try mastering one of these weapons and then move on to another one to experience the satisfaction of bagging hogs using multiple weapons.

The good news is that most of the weapons for hog hunting are relatively affordable. The least expensive of the weapons used for hog hunting can be purchased for around $200 brand new. Of course you could spend a lot more money if you go with high-end brands and get extra features, but to get started and to see if you enjoy the sport there is absolutely no need to let the cost of the weapons prohibit you from hog hunting.

Most common weapons for hog hunting:

- Shotguns

- Rifles

- Bows

Shotguns

Using a shotgun is a very effective way to hunt hogs that are in close range and even on the run. Particularly when hogs are on the run the shotgun is going to a great option, as long as they are close enough to hit. Keep in mind that shotguns typically have an lesser effective range of about 40 - 100 yards, so you need to plan your shots to be within that range. There are some extended range choke tubes that you can buy, and some ammunition available claims to have further killing range, but in most cases you really should plan to be within 100 yards of the hog before shooting.

Even with a shotgun it will be challenging to hit a hog on the run. Not only are they fast, but they quickly change direction when they are running and the areas where you will find hogs can often have many obstructions such as brush or trees in the way. If you are someone who is going to be relying on hog meat as a food source, then a shotgun is a great option. However, if you want to increase the difficulty level of shooting a hog, then you could consider a rifle or bow which I will discuss in a minute.

As far as shotguns, there are two different types to select from. There are semi-automatic and pump shotguns. Semi-automatic shotguns automatically load in the next shell after you shoot so you can take successive shots quickly. However, the downside of a semi-automatic shotgun is the cost. These guns usually start around $700. If you are going to be doing other types of hunting such as waterfowl hunting, the extra cost to invest in a semi-automatic shotgun might be well worth it. I have had a semi-automatic shotgun for three years and truly enjoy the ease with which you can fire multiple rounds.

The other type of shotgun is a pump shotgun. With this shotgun type you must use the pump mechanism to load in the next round each time after you shoot. Although there is definitely an increase in time between shots compared to the semi-automatic shotgun, pump shotguns can be very effective and with some practice you will be able to reload shells quickly. The best part is that pump shotguns are less expensive than semi-automatic shotguns and start around $300 brand new.

You also need to decide what gauge of shotgun to buy. When considering what gauge shotgun you should get, I would recommend a 12-gauge for hog hunting. For chamber size I would recommend a 3-inch chamber. Most shell lengths you will use for hog are 2 ½-inch shells and 2 ¾-inch; however, getting up to a 3-inch chamber gives you some flexibility if you decide to go with a larger shell or if you ever wanted to use the gun for waterfowl hunting. Regarding the barrel length, a 26-inch barrel would work well. This is because it will keep the shot pattern tight enough but it won't be too long for when you are walking around in the woods. You could go up to a 28-inch barrel, but it would just be a little more difficult to maneuver in thick brush and trees.

Rifles

Another choice you could use for hunting hogs is a rifle. There are so many different rifles to choose from it is going to be hard to mention them all but here is a quick list of the different caliber rifles that are commonly used for hog hunting. This is not meant to be an all-inclusive list of rifles you could use, but more a general idea of the great variety of rifles that are commonly used on hogs.

Rifle Calibers Commonly Used for Hog Hunting:

- .17 caliber

- .204 caliber

- .22 caliber

- .223 caliber

- .243 caliber

- .300 caliber

- .308 caliber

Let's discuss the caliber size a little further. Essentially the larger the number for the caliber the larger the bullets are that come out of the gun. For example, a .17 caliber bullet is going to be smaller in diameter than a .308. The larger bullets are going to pack a bigger punch when they hit the hog, but the downside is that the larger bullets can do more damage to the meat and pelt depending on where you hit the hog. In addition, the larger caliber bullets are typically more expensive than bullets for smaller caliber rifles. Also, the cost of the larger caliber guns is typically the highest. This is not always the case based on the exact brand, features and style, but as a general statement that usually holds true.

So what caliber gun should you buy? Well I will first say that if you have access to any of these rifle types you can use them to get into the sport of hog hunting and see what you prefer. I don't think money should get in the way of people having a good time enjoying the outdoors and with such an overabundance of hogs out there we need people hunting them to decrease the population. So you can start off by using what you have, or borrow something from a friend or relative. The benefit of borrowing a rifle is that you get to test it out and see what you prefer before you invest in one.

If you really want the power to drop hogs in their tracks, the larger caliber rifles will be an excellent choice. Again you will typically experience a higher cost for the rifle and ammunition for the larger calibers, but if you have decided that hog hunting is something that you enjoy and are willing to invest in a gun that will work for you to bag many hogs, then go for a larger caliber. Again, a rifle like a .17 or .22 can work, but you may find that the power is not always enough to quickly drop hogs. You may end up taking multiple shots to kill the hog or have times where you wound the hog enough to where it dies eventually, but you have to track it for some distance in order to find it.

Now let's get back to talking about some of the big differences between shotguns and rifles. These differences include effective range and killing radius. First, let's start with killing range. The killing range of a rifle does differ quite a bit based on the caliber and the specific shell that you buy, but some rifles have the ability to shoot hogs up to 200-300 yards away which is quite a long distance. In contrast most shotguns will have an effective range of around 40 yards or so. As you can see if you are planning on taking longer shots at hogs the rifle is going to be the way to go.

However, the downside of hunting with a rifle is the smaller killing radius. With a rifle it is just one bullet that comes out each time you shoot. This means that you really need to be exactly aimed on point with the hog to hit it. Additionally, if the hog is running or if the hog is moving much at all, it will be more challenging to hit them with the single bullet.

When hunting hogs with a rifle you will want to do one of two things in order to hit a hog with a single bullet. First, you could wait until the hog is still. The problem is that not often do hogs stop moving while they are in pursuit of their prey. However, when they do stop rifles are great for shooting hogs. If you do not get a shot at the hog standing still and the hog is now running, then the other way you can be effective in shooting them with a rifle is to be very accurate with your shot placement and pick a specific shooting lane to use. I will discuss shot placement more at a later point in this book, but just be aware that using a rifle will require considerably more shooting accuracy then a shotgun for hogs that are in motion.

Rifles will come in a variety of reloading styles. One is a bolt-action style meaning that you pull a lever back to load or "cock" the gun after you shoot which brings the next bullet into the chamber. Another style is the semi-automatic style which is where the gun automatically reloads itself after each time it is fired, similar to a semi-automatic shotgun. One more style is a pump style where you use a pumping action on the mid-section of the gun to reload. Typically the semi-automatic rifles are the most expensive where the pump and bolt actions are a little lower in cost.

Accessories to consider for your guns

The most obvious accessory that you will need for your gun is the shells but there are many other accessories that you should consider for hog hunting such as scopes, slings, extended-capacity magazines, and tripods. These accessories can make your hog hunting experience more enjoyable and effective.

Accessories to consider for rifles:

- Scopes

- Slings

- Extended-Capacity Magazines

- Tripods

Scopes

If you do plan on hunting hogs with a rifle you may want to consider investing in a scope. A scope is similar to binoculars where it helps magnify distances, making far-away objects appear closer. Having a scope is excellent for shooting at hogs that are sitting still and at a long distance. In this case a scope will allow you to place a very accurate shot on your hog. However, one of the downsides to a scope is they make moving targets harder to shoot. This is because they magnify all of the surroundings which it makes it disorienting and difficult to find your target that is on the move.

Think of it like trying to watch something through binoculars. When the object is still, binoculars are great to see the item close up. However, if the object is moving it can be hard to locate it and keep track of where the object is. The other downside can be their cost. Entry level scopes start around $50 or so, but if you are looking for a scope that has further distance abilities and other features you could easily be looking at several hundred dollars.

Slings

If you have a long walk to your hunting location a sling can be a great way to make carrying your gun easier. Basically, a sling is a strap that attaches to both ends of your gun and goes over your shoulder to free up your hands. This allows you to carry other items and makes it easier to go over some of the difficult terrain you might encounter outdoors.

Slings are usually inexpensive ranging from about $10-$30 and you can purchase them from any sporting goods store. To use a sling, your gun will need to have sling mounts. Basically these are round metal knobs that have holes through them where you can attach your sling. Slings will have a fastening system that slides easily through these holes. If you have a gun that does not have sling mounts you can go to a gunsmith and they can add them to your gun for about $30.

Extended-Capacity Magazines

Some guns have the option to add an extended-capacity magazine. Basically, these serve the purpose of allowing you to hold more bullets in the magazine than what is possible with the standard magazine that the gun comes with. These are primarily used for rifles and are not generally offered for shotguns but can be found with some searching.

The standard capacity of a magazine for most rifles is usually around 5-6 bullets. However, with an extended-capacity magazine they could hold anywhere from 10 to 20 bullets or even more. When you are taking several shots at hogs these extended-capacity magazines can be very convenient. These are particularly useful if you have a semi-automatic rifle as you can make many shots in just a few seconds.

Tripods

When you are hunting with rifles it is important to be able to hold your gun steady for an accurate shot at hogs. One way to accomplish this is to buy a tripod for your rifle. Basically a tripod is made up of two small plastic arms that attach to the bottom of your rifle allowing you to place the rifle on the ground and use these arms to steady the gun in position as you shoot. Tripods work well for steadying your gun if you plan on shooting from a lying down position.

For those of you who want to shoot from a sitting or standing position a rifle stake will be useful, I will discuss rifle stakes in a later section of the book.

Bows

For hunters who are looking to add an additional level of challenge to hog hunting, you should consider hunting with a bow. Bow hunting has been around for ages and used for taking a variety of game animals. Recently bows have become quite popular for hog hunting. Part of this increase in popularity in the use of bows for hog hunting is the increase in the number of people using bows for hunting big game. Now that more people already have a bow for big game hunting, they find it is exciting to use it in other hunting too.

Your range for shooting hogs with a bow is going to be significantly less than compared to a rifle and typically a bit less than with a shotgun as well. For the highest probability shots with a bow you should plan on being within about 20-40 yards of the hog. Due to how close you have to be in order to shoot a hog with a bow, it can really make for an exciting but challenging experience.

Another challenge to mention about using a bow is the learning curve. Learning to use a bow and learning to shoot at distances accurately will typically take someone much longer than it would with a shotgun or rifle. People often practice months or even years before they get to be even average at shooting effectively with a bow. In contrast, most people could learn to shoot a gun well enough to hit a still animal with just a few hours or a few days of practice.

However, after pointing out the downsides of bow hunting, I do not want you to be discouraged with the thought of using a bow for hog hunting. As I have already mentioned it can be a very thrilling experience to hunt with a bow because you are going to be much closer to the hogs for shooting and that can be very exciting. In addition, many people like bow hunting because of the personal satisfaction that they get from using this more challenging way of hunting versus a rifle or shotgun. Rifles and shotguns are great weapons but you really do have a significant advantage over the game you hunt with them because of some of the killing distances you can achieve with them. Using a bow levels the playing field with hogs and thus increases personal satisfaction when you can successfully bag a hog using this method.

Now let's examine how to stay safe and legal…

Step 3: Licensing, Hunter Safety and Rules

Make Sure you Have the Proper Licenses and Any Applicable Safety Registration

It is important to make sure you have the proper licensing and learn hunting safety prior to heading out for a hog hunting adventure. The laws and regulations for hog hunting are very different from one area to the next. The benefit of hunting nuisance animals such as hogs is that in many areas you may not need to purchase a hunting license to be able to hunt hogs. Of course you will want to check your state's regulations to ensure that you are fully compliant with applicable laws. Additionally, you might still need to have some type of safety certification regardless of whether a license is required to hunt hogs or not.

Legal aspects to consider before hunting:

- Area you are hunting

- Specific hunting dates

- Safety certification

- Hunting rules

Area

When you are going to purchase your hunting license, the first thing you will need to know is what area you plan to hunt. Most hunting licenses are good for the entire state that you purchase the license in, but if you will be hunting in multiple states then you will probably need multiple licenses. Be aware that if you are not a resident of the state you plan to hunt in you will typically pay a higher rate for your license. Sometimes it can be as much as double what it costs for a resident of that state to buy a license.

You should also consider what other type of hunting or fishing you plan to do within that year before you buy a hunting license. Some states allow you to purchase a combination license that will give you hunting and fishing privileges for a slightly discounted rate. Not only do you save money this way but it also helps reduce the amount of paperwork you need to carry with you.

Hunting Dates

In addition to knowing what areas you plan to hunt hogs, you will also need to know the dates you plan to hunt them. Just be sure you understand the regulations to ensure that you are covered during the dates that you plan to hunt. Unfortunately, not knowing the rules is not a valid excuse if a game warden catches you without proper licensing. The penalties can be very harsh for people who violate the rules including loss of hunting privileges and confiscation of hunting equipment.

Safety Certification

In addition to having proper licensing, you will also need to ensure that you obtain any necessary safety certifications prior to hunting hogs. Again, the rules in each area are different. In some areas you will need to have a formal safety certification regardless of your age. In other areas if you are over a certain age you do not need to have safety training.

Even if your area does not require any safety training, it is an excellent idea to go through a safety training course prior to doing any type of hunting. Although hunting can be a very fun activity, it also comes with a certain level of safety risk. You can never eliminate all safety risks when hunting, but going through a formal safety class will teach you the skills to improve your safety practices. Hunting safety courses often range from $20 to $100 for a course that will last a few weeks. This is a great investment in your long-term safety.

Rules

There are also a lot of rules to consider when you go hunting for hogs or any other wild game. Some areas have daily limits on the number of hogs you can kill and have in your possession, so make sure you know these rules before going out. There also might be rules concerning your ability to sell the hog pelts. Again, I cannot stress enough the importance of taking some time to read and understand all hunting regulations for your area before hunting hogs.

Now let's take a look at the different seasons for hog hunting...

Step 4: Hunting Seasons

Enjoy the Opportunities Created By Each Season

One of the biggest benefits of hog hunting is that in most areas it can be done year round. This is because hogs are typically considered nuisance animals and it is beneficial to the ecosystem to have as many of them harvested as possible.

For avid hog hunters this is a huge benefit. Each time of year does have its benefits, but each time of year can also present some challenges. Let's take a look at the different seasons for hog hunting and what each provides for hunting excitement. Keep in mind this is a generic description of the season and can vary from region to region.

Seasons:

- Spring

- Summer

- Fall

- Winter

Spring

In the spring of the year you are going to be hunting hogs that have been dealing with cooler or harsh temperatures and weather for the last several months so this means that the hogs may will be more active during this time. The hogs are looking forward to some bigger meals than what they likely had during the winter months. These factors makes the springtime a great time to hunt hogs.

In addition, food sources become more abundant leading to more feeding opportunities for the hogs. However, this can present a challenge. The reason is that hogs will have lots of feeding places available so you may need to do more searching in order to find exactly what area the hogs are currently feeding in.

Since vegetation is just starting to grow back during this time of year the plants and crops might not yet be at the point where their height will hinder your ability to see hogs as they come out into the open. This is great because you can take advantage of more open spots that hogs may head to as they search for food. When they head to the open spots you should be able to see the hogs much easier and be able to place a clear shot with minimal obstruction.

Summer

One clear benefit of hunting during the summer is the temperature. Regardless of where you are located, this time of year will usually have some warm to moderate temperatures. You could actually be hunting in 70 or 80 degree temperatures if not higher in the summer which would be very comfortable or even hot. Some days you can simply wear a short sleeve shirt with a hunting vest rather than having to deal with a bulky coat.

However, the summer can present a challenge in regards to visibility if you are hunting in the woods or even in fields. Leaves on the trees and full brush can make hunting difficult. During this time of year hogs in the woods will be challenging to see, much less shoot successfully. Additionally, hogs out in fields can be hard to see as well if there are tall crops or grass.

You should consider the summer to be the most challenging time of year due to the visibility challenges but also the impact of the high heat on hogs. The high temperatures can cause hogs to become lazy and not move about nearly as much as they will in moderate and cooler temperatures. Hogs will be using the shade of trees and other cover often during this time of year making it much harder to see them. In contrast, when the temperatures are more moderate it is common to see hogs lounging around out in fields and wallows where they can eat while remaining cool.

To be successful with summer hunting you will want to plan your hunting location well to ensure that you have clear shooting lanes. For example, it can be effective to place a feeder with bait near an opening in the woods with clear shooting lanes. You may even want to clear a shooting path with a chainsaw or mower so as soon as hogs come out of the woods or surrounding fields you can take advantage of the shooting lane to bag your hogs.

Another place to hunt in the summer is near water. The heat will cause the hogs to stay close to water and visit watering holes often. Try finding a hunting spot where you have some good visibility and wait for the hogs to come out for a drink. When they do, you should be in a good spot to bag a hog.

One final benefit of hunting in the summer is the less competition that you will likely have with other hog hunters. There is a significantly lower amount of people who hunt in the summer compared to the other seasons because this time of year is more challenging. However, this can be a benefit to you as the hogs are not being pressured by other hunters so those few hogs that are ready to come out into the open may not be as leery. Additionally, if you are seeking private land to hunt, you may not have as many hunters to compete with to get permission to hunt the property.

Fall

As the year progresses into the fall it becomes easier to see hogs in the woods and fields. In many areas in late September and early October the leaves will be falling off the trees and the shrubs and brush on the ground will thin out which will help create better visibility. This makes the fall one of the best times of year to shoot hogs. Additionally, you benefit because the temperatures are a little cooler compared to the summer but probably not cold enough to be uncomfortable yet.

Winter

The winter season will usually present significantly lower temperatures. Depending on where you live temperatures could even dip below zero. In addition to the lower temperatures, you may also have to deal with snow. However, the snow can be helpful in locating hogs as this will enable you to see their tracks on the ground. To deal with these temperatures ensure that you dress appropriately with a thick coat and winter boots. Layers are also good as you can remove clothes if you get too warm.

At this time of year you will typically have the benefit of very clear areas in the woods. Most trees will be free of leaves and there will be less vegetation on the ground, enabling you to see hogs better. The shooting opportunities will greatly increase with this greater visibility. Snow on the ground for tracking hog movement and for finding wounded hogs after shooting them is also a great benefit of late winter hunting.

However, these clear shooting opportunities do present an equal challenge for you. This is because you will also not have as many places to hide effectively so you will need to ensure that you plan your cover well during this season. You should also plan to match your surrounding such as the snow. Many times the winter hunts will be with snow around you so put on white camouflage or a white ghillie suit to blend in well. Additionally, the winter can be a perfect time to use a hunting blind for concealment as well as protection from the elements.

Another benefit of hunting in the winter is some areas extend the hunting hours of hogs into the evening or all night. Additionally, the laws may loosen further during these times including the use of night hunting equipment such as spotlights, night vision scopes and other night hunting equipment. All of these tools would greatly improve your chances of bagging hogs in the winter.

Now lets learn how to successfully scout for hogs...

Step 5: Scouting for Success & Looking for Signs of Hogs

How to Select the Proper Location to Hunt Hog

As with most hunting the more time you invest finding the spots where your game is located, the higher the chances are that you will be successful when you head out for the actual hunt. This holds true with hog hunting as well. Let's take a look at some places to go hog hunting.

Identifying Areas for Hog Hunting:

- Pay attention to where you see hogs

- Call for hogs when scouting

- Prairies and fields

- Near farm pastures

- Woods

- Near water

- Use trail cameras

- Look for tracks

- Observe for droppings

Pay Attention to Where you See Hogs

This should be obvious but you want to pay attention to where you see hogs. When you are driving around keep an eye out in the fields and woods and actively look for hogs. If you often see hogs in a certain area this should be a great place for you to start. Also, you can ask your friends and family to be on the lookout for you. Let them know that you want to go hog hunting and ask if they could pay attention to what they are seeing. It is better to have several people searching for hogs rather than doing it alone and often friends and family will be willing to help you out with this.

Another strategy to get the feedback of others on good places to hunt is to make a posting to your favorite social media website and let people know that you are looking to go hog hunting. Ask and see if your friends have suggestions on where to go. This is a great way to get the word out to a lot of people at once and often people will be willing to help you out and provide some ideas. If people do not know that you want to hunt hogs there is no way they can help you out. You may be pleasantly surprised with the success you have in finding a spot for hog hunting when you simply ask for help.

Call for Hogs When Scouting

When you are out driving around looking for a hunting spot, I would recommend that you bring your hog calls with you. Even if you are not planning to hunt that day, you can use this as an opportunity to test your calling and see if you get any responses from hogs in the area. Step out of your vehicle and set up your electronic caller (electronic and mouth callers will be discussed in depth later) or start calling on your mouth call. Do this for a good 10-20 minutes to see if you can get any response from nearby hogs or if any hogs approach. If you are able to get a response or have hogs approach in this short period of time you have likely found a hunting spot that is worth coming back to when it is actually time for your hunting trip.

Prairies and Fields

Open prairies and fields are some of the absolute best places to hunt for hogs. These open areas are excellent hunting grounds for the hogs as they search for food and water to wallow in. This in turn makes for good hunting spots for you because as the hogs are out searching for their food and watering holes you can be out searching for the hogs. In addition, prairies and fields are good for hunting because you usually have great viewing distances to spot those hogs. Try to find the higher spots to sit because they will give you increased viewing distance as hogs come out of hiding.

Near Farm Pastures

Since hogs are opportunistic feeders, the pastures near farms can be excellent hunting locations for hogs. They may eat food that is placed out for the farm animals or even garbage that could be near this area. Of course if you have asked a farmer to hunt their land and they have given you permission they should be able to tell you where a good area is to find hogs on their property. Who else would be better to tell you where the hogs are located then the landowner themselves.

Another benefit of being near farm pastures is that these areas typically provide a lot of options for you to hide as you wait for hogs. For example, you might be able to station yourself in one of the windows on a barn and have excellent viewing distance from this elevated spot. In addition, there are usually some farm machines or other buildings that you could sit next to in order to stay out of the sight of hogs.

Woods

Although woods are a good place to find hogs, woods are also a challenging place to shoot hogs. The trees, branches and leaves can make it challenging to see hogs in this type of environment. Once a hog starts running in the woods you will have minimal time to be able to shoot it. They run very fast and the further they get from you, the more branches and leaves that will be in your shooting lane.

When hunting in the woods, it is best to try to find an area that has a clearing. This will allow you to have a little more of an opportunity to shoot at the hogs without much in the way. Areas where you hunt for hogs are often the same areas where people hunt for deer or other wild game. The great thing about hunting in an area that is used for deer hunting is that there are likely going to be some deer hunting stands that you could use to sit in for hunting hogs. Anytime you can get to a high spot, you are put at an advantage as you can see longer distances. In addition, by being elevated you are out of the direct line of sight of the hogs (I will discuss stands and concealment later).

Near Water

All animals need to drink water at some point which means that setting up near water you are likely in a spot where you will eventually see some hogs. Ponds, rivers, lakes and streams are some areas where it will be common to find hogs drinking. In addition, hogs know that they will have a good opportunity to find fresh vegetation near the water. In the winter any open water spots can be even more of a prime spot for hunting because if most water has frozen over, the few spots that are open and easily accessible are going to be highly frequented by both hogs.

Use Trail Cameras

A fun way to validate that there are hogs in the area you plan to hunt is to utilize trail cameras. Basically a trail camera is a camera that you can attach to a tree, fencepost or other stationary item that captures pictures when there is motion in the area. You affix the trail camera by wrapping the straps around the stationary object at a height that will pick up the image you are trying to get.

Trail camera technology has come a long way and it is truly amazing what you can do with them now. Many trail cameras operate with a memory card where you insert a memory card and any pictures that are taken are stored on the card. You can then view these images on a computer or even some mobile phones can pull images from the memory card. In recent years they have come up with trail cameras that work with an internet connection so any images that are taken are sent directly to your mobile phone for instant viewing. This is really great because it saves you the time and money of driving to the camera location to check the memory card. However, the downside is the trail cameras with this feature are significantly more expensive than the standard memory card style.

Look for Tracks

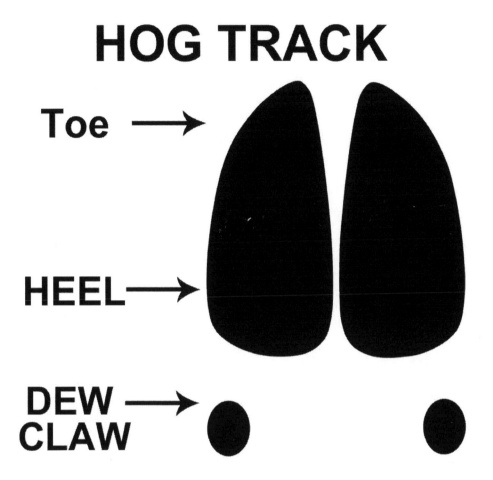

Another sure fire way to know if there are hogs in the area is to look for hog tracks left on the ground. However, you may not see these unless there is soft ground or there is snow on the ground. Hunting for hogs in the snow will be one of the best times to be able to see where hogs are traveling from the footprints they leave behind in the snow. Note that their footprints will vary in size based on the size of the hog. Many hogs will have footprints about 2 -3 inches in length by about 1.5 to 2 inches wide. The prints consist of a base hoof print and sometimes you can see the two dew claw prints which can resemble two two ovals or two partial triangle shapes facing out depending on how the hog stepped.

Observe for Droppings

Another indicator of hogs in the area is their droppings. Hog droppings are the shape of small stones such as agates with irregular shaping and are up to about 4 inches long. Their composition can vary greatly based on what they recently ate but they are typically it could be black and smooth in color.

As you walk through the woods be sure to take time to not only observe the ground for prints but also look for droppings on the ground. If you find a pile of droppings you should stop to examine them. If the droppings have a wet appearance then that means that the droppings are fresh and that the hog was in the area recently. When the droppings have a dried out appearance that means they are older but it can still be a good sign that hogs may still be living nearby.

Now let's discuss how to get permission to hunt private land...

Step 6: Getting Permission to Hunt Private Land

Tips for Asking Permission

If you are like me, you do not own hunting land and don't always want to battle other hunters for public land. In addition, many fields prime for hog hunting are often private property. At first it can feel a little uncomfortable to ask other people to use their land for hog hunting. However, after some experience the process gets much easier. Also, if you get permission to hunt on someone's land one time, they are likely to let you come back again in the future. It can also be advantageous to some property owners to have you hunt their land if they want to thin out the hog population that might be damaging livestock feeding areas or being a nuisance on their property.

Tips to get permission to hunt private land:

- Don't be afraid to ask

- Don't wear hunting clothes when approaching them to ask

- Be kind and smile

- Bring a youth hunter if possible

- Tell them exact times you will be there

- Do a favor in return

- Bring them meat or another gift

- Thank them after

Don't Be Afraid to Ask

Something that holds hunters back from finding land to hunt is the fear of asking for permission. People can feel intimidated by asking landowners for permission to hunt on their property. But the more you do it, the more you get used to it. When you are turned down for permission the primary reason is usually that they already have a friend or family member that hunts the area.

Additionally, I would say that you have a greater chance of getting permission to hunt private property for hogs compared to nearly any other type of game animal. For example, if you ask people to hunt deer on their property it may be possible that they hunt deer themselves or have family members or friends who hunt deer. With hogs, not as many people hunt them and if they are deer hunters they are going to want to get the hogs off their property to preserve the deer habitat.

Sample wording to use when asking permission:

- Hello, my name is ___ and I am hoping to do some hog hunting tomorrow. It seems like you have a great piece of land for hog hunting. Would it be okay with you if I hunted on your property this weekend?

- Good afternoon, I am looking for a place to hog hunt with my friend tomorrow. Would it be possible for us to hunt on your land for hogs for a few hours in the morning?

- Hello, I was driving by your property on my way to town last night and I saw a hog in your field. I really enjoy hog hunting and I'm wondering if it would be okay with you if I could hunt here for a few hours tonight.

If they say no, don't waste this opportunity to find a hunting spot. Thank them and ask them if they know of any other places nearby that they would suggest trying. They might know another landowner that would allow you to hunt their property or they might know of some good public land for hunting in the area.

Don't Wear Hunting Clothing

I recommend not wearing hunting clothing when you go to ask for permission to hunt on someone's property because it can give the landowners a feeling that you are assuming that you will be able to hunt there. Not all people like or allow hunting so don't assume anything. If you are planning on hunting that same day, at least take off your camouflage clothing. It should not take too much to remove the items that make you look like a hunter. If you are dressed like you are ready to hunt, it can also give them the impression that you may go hunt on their land even if they do not give you permission.

Be Kind and Smile

This should go without saying but if you are polite to the landowner they will more than likely be polite back. Be conscious when you approach the property to put a smile on your face to ensure that you are received as a friendly individual. Do what you can to strike up a conversation with the landowner by asking them some questions such as how long they have lived at the property or what they do for a living. People love to talk about themselves so if you can get the conversation going and let the landowner talk, it will likely improve your chances of getting permission to hunt their land. If they do agree to allow you to hunt on their property, keep the conversation going and ask them where on their property in particular they would recommend hunting. After all, they should know best where the hogs have been on their property.

Bring a Youth Hunter

Most people have a soft spot for children so if you are planning to hunt with a child it can help to bring them with you when you ask for permission. People who would have said no to you alone may say yes if it means that a child will get the opportunity to experience the outdoors. Another benefit of bringing a child is that it can be a great learning experience for the child. This helps get the child used to speaking to strangers and helps them learn all of the aspects of hunting that will be valuable to them when they start hunting on their own.

Tell Them the Exact Times You Will Be There

To help put the landowners at ease, it is important to let them know exactly when you plan to hunt. If you want to hunt just one morning, tell them that. Or if you want access for an entire weekend, be specific so they are not taken off guard when they see you on their property. This is very important because people will feel more comfortable knowing the exact times that they can expect to see you rather than having you show up at any random time of the day. Never go hunting on someone else's property at a time when you do not have permission.

Do a Favor In Return

Landowners often have work that needs to be done around their property, particularly if they are farmers. Ask them if there are a few projects that you could help out with for an afternoon or two in exchange for hunting on their property. Not only would assisting with these chores be a way to get permission to hunt, it is also a great way to form a relationship with the landowner. The more you get to know them, the more likely they are to let you to continue to hunt there.

Bring Them Meat or Other Small Gifts

Another thing you can ask is if the landowners would like to have some meat in exchange for allowing you to hunt there. Even if they don't hunt, people may like getting some free meat. This can be a great win-win situation for both parties. If they don't like like hog meat you could bring some other type of meat that you have harvested to share with them. Maybe you hunted deer earlier in the year and have leftover venison. If you do, you could bring them a pack or two of the meat to thank them for allowing you to hunt there.

Additionally, other small gifts could be a way to say thank you to the landowner for allowing you to use their property. You could bake some cookies in advance or stop at the store on the way and buy some cookies to give them. It does not have to be anything very expensive but something simple can go a long way in letting them know that you appreciate their generosity in allowing you to hunt on their property.

Benefits of Getting Permission Effectively

If you follow these steps and are respectful with those who allow you to hunt their land, you may end up with one or more long-term hunting spots. Be kind when asking, do something in return, and get to know the landowners. The better the connections you make with people, the more likely you will be to build a great network of landowners and have multiple hunting locations that you can use.

Our next section covers finding public land for hog hunting...

Step 7: Finding Public Land to Hunt

Public Land Can Provide Excellent Hunting Opportunities

Similar to private land, with some effort you can find some great hunting spots available on public land. Again, if you are like me and do not own land to hunt and you have not had any luck getting permission to hunt private land, then you may want to look into finding public land to hunt.

Types of public lands available for hunting hogs:

- Wildlife Management Areas (WMAs)

- State Forests

- Wildlife Refuges

- National Forests

- County Land

Tips about using public land:

- Search online

- Contact your state wildlife office

- Scout out the area in advance

- Be safe

Search Online

With a little online research you will be sure to find some public hunting land within a reasonable driving distance from your home. Simply search online using any of the terms listed above under "Types of public land available for hunting hogs" followed by your state or county name and there will be sure to be a listing. Each state has different regulations for these areas so if you have questions regarding hunting regulations that are not clearly denoted online, be sure to reach out to your state wildlife office directly.

Contact Your State Wildlife Office

State wildlife officers are usually very friendly people and passionate about the outdoors. Don't be afraid to call the wildlife office and ask them what areas they would suggest nearby for hog hunting. They want to help people enjoy the outdoors so if you ask, they are going to be happy to assist. Additionally, they understand the importance of properly managing the hog population in preservation of a healthy environment so they will likely be motivated to help you find a place to hunt hogs.

Scout the Area in Advance

Once you have a site in mind, if possible, it is great to scout out the area in advance. Try driving to the hunting location a few days prior to actually hunting and review the territory. Take a walk and note if you see any hogs. Even if you are unable to physically go to the hunting spot in advance, you can use online resources to help you plan your hunt. Since you may have found this location by looking online for public hunting areas, you can usually find online maps for these public lands. Scan those maps to determine where you will hunt and the route you will take to your hunting spot in advance.

Safety

Safety is the primary thing to be aware of when hunting on public land. Since it is public land, anyone can use this land and there is no way to guarantee that you are alone. It is important to check your surroundings before you shoot. You may find it easy to get caught up in the excitement of shooting and forget what is around you. However, you first want to think about what is in the direction you are shooting as bullets can travel a long distance. You need to be one hundred percent sure that there is nobody in the vicinity that could possibly get hit. If you are ever in doubt if you have a safe shot, do not shoot.

Now let's look how to use bait to attract hogs…

Step 8: Baiting to Improve your Odds

Use Bait to Lure Hogs within Shooting Range

Something that can be a huge benefit to your hog hunting success is implementing bait into your hunting strategy. Consistently placing bait in an area that you want the hogs to come to helps train the animals to find food in that spot. Then when you are ready to hunt that spot you should have a pretty good chance of bagging some hogs.

What to use as bait:

- Store Bought Bait

- Corn

- Big game carcasses

- Butcher scrap

- Dog food

- Fish carcasses

Store Bought Bait

One of the easiest forms of bait for hogs is to buy hog bait from a store. There are wide range of baits that are available for hog hunting so you will likely have several choices when you head to the local sporting goods stores. These pre made baits are often plump full of sugary substances that pigs love and blended with smells that pigs will pick up from a long distance away. However, the downside of store bought bait is the cost as 5 pound bags can start around $10 and go way up from there depending on the quantity you need as well as the specific formula of that bait. Hog hunters looking for a grab and go bait may find the investment worth it in hunting success as well as time saved.

Corn

Using corn as hog bait is typically lower cost compared to store bought hog bait. This is because a large sack of corn can often be purchased in much higher quantities for significantly lower prices. A good idea is to check local granaries for corn bags as well as feed stores for good deals. To boost up the luring ability of your corn you may want to add some ingredients to it. For example, adding sugar, beer, Kool aid and syrup are just a few ideas of things to add that will make hogs go crazy for your corn bait.

Big Game Carcasses

Many hog hunters also hunt other animals including big game. If you are reading this it is likely that you may have hunted big game in the past so I recommend that you try and use the carcasses from your big game hunts for hog meat. Even if you do not hunt big game yourself you may know someone who does. Most people really have no use for a big game carcass so if you let your friends know that you want the carcasses of any game they bag they are probably going to be willing to help you out.

Butcher Scrap

Another way to get some hog bait is to check with your local butcher and see if you can get leftover scrap meat from them. Butchers usually end up throwing away the fat and some trimmings that are just not edible to humans so they may be willing to help you out. Even if they want to charge a few dollars for the scraps it is likely going to be a lot less expensive than going out and buying other forms of hog bait.

Dog Food

Another good and inexpensive bait to try for hogs is dog food. My recommendation is to go a discount store to find dog food. The dog food does not need to be anything fancy. In fact I would buy the cheapest bag that you can find in bulk and you should be set. The nice thing with dog food is it is something that you can easily throw in a container in the back of your vehicle and then you can put some out in several places near your hunting spot as you prep the area for hogs. It is something that is not going to stink up your vehicle like some other forms of hog bait might.

Fish Carcasses

Many areas of the country have some type of fishing that happens and if you are a sports person you might go fishing as well as hog hunting. The next time you are out fishing, hang onto the leftover carcasses after you clean the fish and use that as bait for hog hunting. Of course you will want to keep this in a sealed bag outside to keep the smell out of your house, or bring it right away to your hunting spot. Since the smell of dead fish is very potent, the hogs will be able to smell this bait from a long way away.

Baiting Tips

Once you have decided what you are going to use as bait, it is time to plan how and when you are going to bait for hogs. Ideally, you want to bait the hogs for several days prior to the day that you actually plan to hunt. For example, if you plan to hog hunt on Saturday, you would ideally want to start baiting them by Tuesday or Wednesday of that week so the hogs get used to the bait for at least a few days in advance.

In addition, you want to try to bait around the same time that you plan on hunting. This is because the hogs are going to get used to finding food at that specific time so you should plan on being there at this time as well. For example, if you always bait in the late afternoon then I would suggest that you plan on hunting in the late afternoon after several days of baiting.

To make baiting easier many hog hunters opt to use corn feeders for storing and releasing their bait. Corn feeders are often used for baiting other game as well such as deer and can easily be swapped out for your hog baiting use. Many corn feeders have a slow feed release method so not all of the bait is eaten at once. This is an advantage over just putting out a pile of bait out on the ground where it would all likely be eaten quickly, possibly before you are back out for your hunting trip.

Now let's look at some items to consider bringing with you on your hunt…

Step 9: Field Essentials

Bring These Additional Items for Hunting Hogs

Earlier we discussed gun types and accessories for hog hunting. Now let's take a look at some of the other items that you may want to bring with you on your hunting trip.

Other items to bring hunting:

- Shooting stick

- Hunting knife

- Compass

- Flashlight

- Food and water

- Thermal scope / night vision goggles

Shooting Stick

When taking long distance shots it can be useful to use a shooting stick to help balance your rifle for the most accurate shot possible. A shooting stick is basically a plastic or metal stick that has a "V" opening on the top side. What you do is rest the barrel of your gun in the opening of the "V" and then you hold the rest of your gun as you normally would. You are still able to easily move back and forth behind the shooting stick as you track the hog in your sights. Once the hog is within effective shooting range and the hog has stopped moving, you can pull the trigger and hopefully get a well-placed shot on the hog.

If you hunt without a shooting stick it is a little more difficult to hold your gun up in the air for long periods of time while you wait for the hog to be in good shooting position. Your arms are likely to get tired while waiting for the hog to stop and this might result in you having to lower the gun and rest your arms for a moment. However, this creates extra movement and there is a chance the hog could spot you moving. With the shooting stick it will reduce arm fatigue as you can rest the majority of the weight of the gun on the stick. In addition, you benefit because the stick is going to hold your gun stable. Holding your gun without a stick makes it harder to keep perfectly still because as you breathe the gun can move slightly. However, with a stick, the gun will be in a stable position the entire time.

Hunting Knife

A hunting knife is an important tool that you will want to bring with on your hog hunting adventure. After you shoot a hog you will need a knife to be able to clean it and remove the entrails and prep the meat. Make sure that you sharpen your knife before you go hunting because a sharp knife makes cutting easier. Surprisingly a sharp knife adds to your safety too because you won't have to push so hard to cut which will reduce the chances of the knife slipping and you cutting yourself.

Compass

Depending on the location you are going to hunt and how familiar you are with the area you are in, it can be a great idea to bring a compass with you. Any time that you are hunting a new area you should bring a compass for safety. The chances of getting lost are pretty slim but it is better to have one with you to be safe. Especially if you are going to hunt on public land that you have not hunted before it would be a good idea to bring a compass. If you have a compass app on your phone that would work great so you don't have to carry an additional item with you. However, the downside is many compass apps require reception so if you are in a remote area without reception they will be useless. The other risk is if your phone runs out of battery power you will now be without a compass.

Flashlight

If you will be hunting early in the morning or into the evening hours, it is best to bring a flashlight with you in case you are traveling to and from your hunting site in the dark. It is best to limit your use of the flashlight as much as possible because the hogs can spot the light from a long way away, but depending on the area you are hunting it may be necessary to use one to find your hunting spot.

Food and Water

It is very important to bring some water and food with you on your hunting trip. When you are going to hunt for just an hour or so, a bottle of water and a snack bar should get you through. Having just this little bit of food and water can help keep you hydrated and energized. When you plan longer trips you may want to bring a few bottles of water and even pack a lunch. Without food and water you might have to stop hunting sooner than you want. With some food and water you can extend your hunting trip, particularly on those days when you are having good success.

Thermo Scope / Night Vision Goggles

If you really have some money to throw into this sport you may consider purchasing night vision goggles or a thermo scope for night hunts. Goggles and scopes with night vision can be very useful to see hogs when it is dark and will make evening hunting even more productive as it reduces the challenge of no light. However, the biggest downside is going to be the cost. You could easily spend several hundred dollars if not several thousand dollars on night vision optics.

Now let's examine what to do as soon as you arrive at your hunting spot...

Step 10: Arriving at your Hunting Spot

Your Chances of Success Start as Soon as You Arrive at Your Hunting Spot

It is extremely important to be aware of every little detail when you are about to arrive at your hunting spot and as you walk to the spot where you plan on hunting. Hogs are wary and will notice things that are out of the ordinary and will do their best to keep a good distance away from humans.

Pay Attention to Little Details to Have Hog Hunting Success:

- Arrival Path
- Noise

Arrival Path

To start off with, it is a good idea to park a good distance away from your hunting location. Hogs are able to see and hear vehicles approaching, so be sure that you park your vehicle at least several hundred yards away from the location you plan to hunt. Although it is not always fun to walk a long distance, your hunting success can be greatly compromised when parking near your hunting spot.

As you walk from your vehicle to your hunting location you should also pay attention to your cover along the way. What I mean is that you should try and stay as concealed as much as possible as you make your way to the hunting pot. For example, you are often going to be hunting out in fields or other open areas. These open areas are great because you can see the hogs from a good distance away without much obstruction when you want to aim and shoot.

However, these open areas also present the same clear line of sight for. So you must keep this in mind to improve your hunting success. Most fields are going to have some type of tree line or taller grass or vegetation along the edges of the field. By walking along these, the natural cover you will keep you a little more concealed rather than blatantly walking across an open field. Of course there is no way to walk to a hunting spot without any chance of being spotted, but being aware of movement you are making can help reduce the chances of alerting nearby hogs.

WALKING TO YOUR HUNTING SPOT

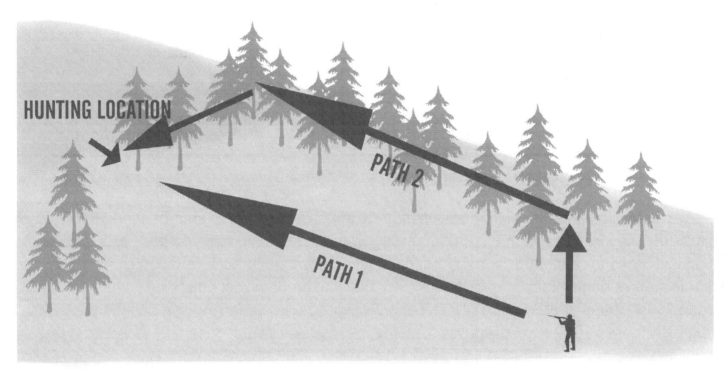

As you can see in the illustration above there are two paths that you could use to walk to the hunting location, path 1 or path 2. In the example the hunting location is towards the top of the hill and the hunter plans to hunt from underneath a few trees there as it should give clear shooting lanes and long viewing distances. Path 1 shows the clearest and easiest path to get to your destination. This is because anytime you are trying to get somewhere the shortest way to go is in a straight line. Additionally, since this is an open field there is not much in your way so you will likely not be stepping over fallen down trees, battling thick brush or have much difficult terrain to navigate.

However, path 1 has a significant downside in getting to your hunting spot and that is the fact that you will be out in the open for a long period of time while you are walking. This entire time you will be exposed to the sight of any nearby hogs and you will likely scare them away making your long walk entirely wasted. However, what you can do to reduce the chances of being spotted is use path 2. As you can see with path 2 there is a tree line that the hunter is going to walk along to stay concealed. He is going to walk several yards into the tree line to use the trees as a natural covering to conceal his movement and body. Path 2 is longer in distance, uphill, and likely has more vegetation to get through making for a more challenging walk, but ultimately choosing this path over path 1 can be beneficial.

Of course the illustration is just an example of how you can get to your hunting spot and reduce your chances of being seen. The area you are going to hunt is most likely going to be different, but this section is to help you understand the concept that it is best to stay out of wide open spaces as you walk to your hunting spot for hog hunting. Even though finding paths with more cover are likely to take longer and may be more difficult to navigate, staying out of the sight of hogs can help keep from scaring the hogs away.

Noise

Another consideration to keep in mind as you arrive at your hunting spot is controlling the amount of you noise you make. Of course it is pretty much impossible to eliminate all noise, but being aware of the noise you are making and doing as much as you can to reduce it will decrease the chances that you scare away hogs. Hogs do have a very good hearing so every little bit you do in reducing noise makes a difference.

Be aware of these noise makers:

- Shutting vehicle doors

- Talking

- Stepping on sticks/leaves

- Loading weapons

- Setting up decoys, bait and electronic callers

Next we will look at how important wind and sun are to hog hunting...

Step 11: Sun Impact

Using The Sun to Your Advantage

One tactic you can implement to improve your hog hunting success is utilizing the sun to help keep yourself concealed from hog. It's important to do anything you can in order to reduce chances of being spotted by hogs. This means that the sun can play a key factor in hog hunting success.

First off, the sun can be blinding to you as you try and see hogs. So let's say that you have setup in a way in which the sunrise is going to be coming directly from the direction that you are looking, the East. This is going to make it difficult for you to see hogs as you will be blinded by the bright sun shining directly into your face.

The second reason is that hogs are impacted in a similar manner to humans by the bright light of the sun. When hogs walk directly into the sun, it is more challenging for them to see every little detail that is out in front of them due to the bright light. The great thing is that you can use this to your benefit because if you setup with the sun at your back the hogs will be forced to look into the sun and this can reduce the chances of you being spotted. So as a general rule of thumb setup with the sun to your back and be setup in the shade.

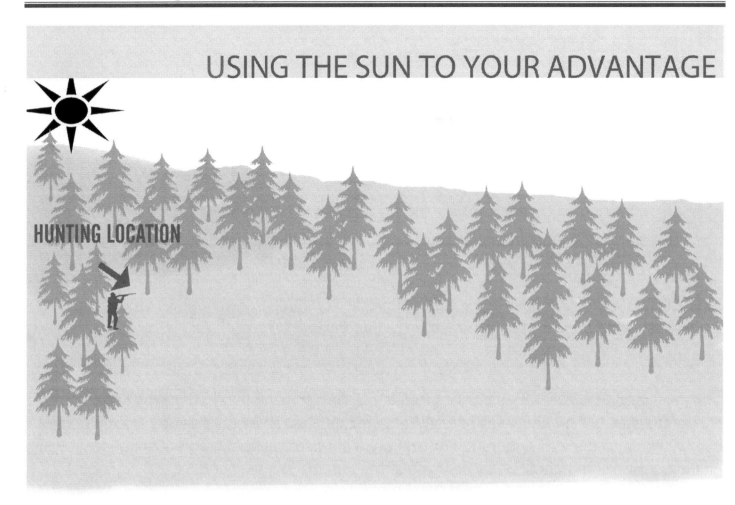

USING THE SUN TO YOUR ADVANTAGE

HUNTING LOCATION

This above example shows how the sun can be of benefit to you as a hog hunter. You can see that the sun is to the left of the image which means the sun is at the hunters back. As the hog approaches, they will be looking in the direction that the sun is shining from and that can hinder their ability to see anything out in front of them.

USING THE SUN TO YOUR ADVANTAGE

In this example I want to show you what to try and avoid in regards to sun. You will now notice is the sun is on the right side of the image. This means that the hunter will be looking directly at the sun as the hog approaches. Looking in the direction of the sun can be blinding and make it challenging to see the approaching hogs. When it is possible you want to try and setup with the sun at your back.

Now let's take a look at how wind impacts your hunting...

Step 12: Wind Impact

Using Wind to Your Advantage

In addition to using the sun as an advantage to your hog hunting you should also consider how you can use wind to improve your hunting success. With proper knowledge of wind impact, you can use both the wind and sun to your advantage as you work to harvest hogs.

Wind

Something that beginning hog hunters might not be are aware of is how the wind can impact hog behavior and your chances of being noticed by hogs. The basic thing to know about wind when hunting hogs is that wind sends odors in the direction that the wind is blowing. What this means is that any odors that are coming from the upwind side to where hogs are located are likely to be noticed by the hogs.

You must keep this in mind as you hunt because you will typically want to plan on approaching hogs from the downwind side of them. When you approach hogs from the downwind side, the wind will carry your sent away from hogs so unless they see you or hear you while walking closer, your chances of scaring them off before you are able to shoot are going to be significantly decreased.

How to Know What Way the Wind is Coming From?

Sometimes the wind direction will be quite obvious if it is a strong wind. However, there are times when it is a little more challenging to figure out wind direction so here are a few ways you can tell what way the wind is blowing.

- Check your phone weather app for wind indicator; some GPS systems will have a wind indicator as well.

- Look at trees or grass and see which way the leaves and grass are blowing.

- Pull a handful of grass or dirt and hold it about chest high. Slowly let some out of your hands and see which way it blows.

- Buy a "wind checker" bottle. These are small bottles that are filled with a powder, and when you squeeze the bottle, they let a small puff of powder out in the air. You simply observe the direction the powder blows and that will indicate the wind direction. These are sold at many sporting goods stores and online if you search "wind checker bottle" and are just a few dollars.

UNDERSTANDING WIND

WIND DIRECTION >>>

Above is an example to help you visualize what I mean when I say that wind will carry scent to the hogs. As you can see from the illustration, the wind is blowing from left to right so that means that hogs will be able to smell things that are on the left side of the image because the wind is blowing the scent directly at the hog. In this case, the hunter is on the left, so it is likely that the hogs will easily scent the hunter. Now that you understand how hogs use wind to smell out in front of them

UNDERSTANDING WIND

WIND DIRECTION ‹‹‹‹

In this example of wind direction, you can see that the wind is blowing from right to left on the image. This means that the hog is less likely to smell the hunter because now the hunter is on the downwind side of the hog. Any scent that the wind blows from the hunter is going to blow the scent away from the hog. This particular example is an ideal setup because the hog out in front of the hunter is extremely unlikely to scent the hunter. However, you still want to be careful of not being seen or heard by the hogs.

UNDERSTANDING WIND

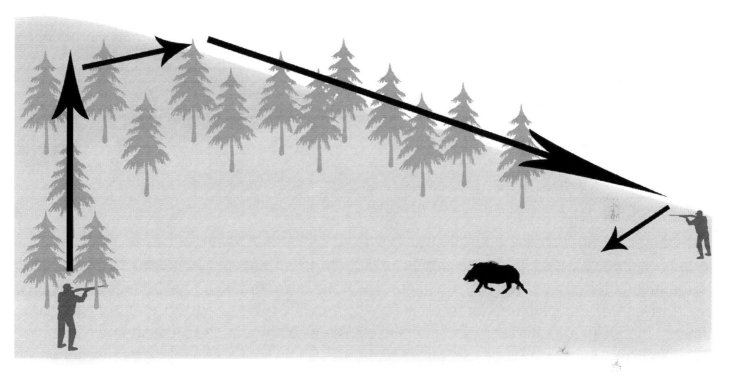

WIND DIRECTION ⟫

In this final example of wind direction for hog hunting I will show you what to do when you find yourself on the upwind side of a hog. As this image shows, the wind is blowing from the hunter directly at the hog so there is a chance the hog will smell the hunter. So if you find yourself in this situation, you will want to try and work yourself to the downwind side of the hog to get a closer shot at the hog and reduce your chances of being scented.

In order to accomplish not being scented in this situation, it would be recommended to walk to the backside of the hill or further to across a field. Then move down the hill on the backside where or further across a field you will not be seen by the hogs. After you make it all of the way around you can then walk back closer where the hog is and work to find a good shooting spot. As you will now be on the downwind side of the hog the chances of you being scented are greatly decreased.

This is a very basic example of using wind to your advantage. However, this concept can be utilized in so many different ways. Really, the trick is to try and always be on the downwind side of where the hogs are. For example, if you have patterned hogs over several days and you know that they are following a certain trail each day you should decide what side of the trail to setup on based on the wind. You will want to setup on the side of the trail where the wind is blowing in your face rather than at your back. With the wind blowing in your face the chances of the hogs smelling you as they walk down the trail is very low.

Scent Cover-Ups

Now that we have discussed how hogs can smell well and that you need to use the wind to your advantage we should also discuss scent cover-ups. There will be times when you are hog hunting that you find yourself in not an ideal spot and your scent may be blowing towards nearby hogs. To be prepared for these times you can use some cover-up scents. There are several manufacturers that sell synthetic and even real hog scent. If you put some of this on your clothing, it can actually help attract hogs or at least help cover up the human scent on you. It is not a bad idea to have some of this to reduce the chances of scaring off hogs.

Now let's discuss how to effectively be concealed to fool hogs…

Step 13: Concealment

Staying Hidden from Hogs is Critical to Success

Hogs, especially older and more experienced ones, are wary and will always be on the lookout for anything that seems out of the ordinary. You must keep this in mind as you determine where you are going to sit and wait for hogs.

Ways to Stay Hidden:

- Hunting blind
- Natural covering
- Deer/tree stands
- Stay out of direct line of sight
- Avoid body silhouette
- Camouflage & face paint
- Scent control

Hunting Blind

A simple yet effective way to stay concealed from the sight of hogs is by using a ground blind. Hog hunting often involves moving to several different spots, so ground blinds are a perfect solution. These blinds are like little tents with zip-open windows for shooting. When hunting from a ground blind you will want to bring some type of chair with you to sit on because sitting on the ground for any length of time will not be comfortable.

One of the biggest benefits of ground blinds is that you can place them in high-traffic areas that do not have much in the way of natural covering around. For example, if there is an open prairie without many trees or shrubs, the blind can be a good option. Simply try to find some type of covering like a small tree or bush and place the blind next to it. The bush itself would not provide you enough cover, but now with the use of the blind you should be hidden well from the hogs.

There are a few other benefits to ground blinds which include the fact that they will keep you out of the elements and comfortable. Like I mentioned, these are like little tents so when it is windy, raining, snowing or cold outside these blinds will help you stay somewhat protected from the elements and much more comfortable during your hunt. The last benefit to mention about ground blinds is their low cost. You can find them on sale at hunting stores for around $40. Of course you can find more expensive ones, but for something to get you started an entry-level blind should do the trick.

Natural Concealment

Utilizing your surroundings to keep you out of the sight of hogs can be another great way for concealment. Often times you will be hunting hogs that are in an open field or prairie. The good thing about hunting fields is that these fields will often be lined with trees, tall grass, fence lines or even woods that you can use to keep hidden.

For example, the field might have a fence line on the side of the field and then some woods on the other side of the fence. This can be a great situation as you could sit below the trees with the fence in front of you as you look out over the field. The fence in front of you should provide some additional cover but you should still have good shooting lanes as hogs run in the fields.

With natural concealment you can get very creative on what to use to keep yourself covered. For example when hunting a prairie that is very hilly, you could lie down on the top of one of the hills with a lot of camouflage on and then look out over the field from this higher elevation. The natural curvature of the hill can help keep you hidden as long as you stay towards the back portion of the crest of the hill so the hill keeps you mostly concealed.

Deer/Tree Stands

The areas that hogs live in are typically areas that deer live in as well. In pretty much any place that has deer there are likely to be some people that hunt deer. A great benefit of this is that deer hunters often use elevated deer stands for hunting and those deer stands can work well for hunting hogs as well. There are a variety of deer stands such as ladder stands (which is pictured above), but people also use tripod stands which are stands that sit on a large tripod style base so they do not need to be placed in a tree.

Regardless of the style of deer stands that are available to you on the land you hunt, these could all be useful for hunting hogs. One clear benefit of using a deer stand is the elevation that it provides you. Many deer stands are 8-15 feet up in the air and by sitting in them it will greatly increase the distance that you will be able to see hogs. Another benefit of being high up in the air is that it takes you out of the direct line of sight of hogs.

Of course if you do use a tree stand you still need to be aware of concealment so you still should have camouflage on and depending on the stand you have it might not provide much to hide your movement. So when you do hunt out of a tree stand it is still important not to move very much because even though you are elevated in the air it is still possible that the hogs could see you, particularly if you are moving around a lot.

Stay out of Direct Line of Sight

Another tactic to keep in mind when hunting hogs is to be sure that you stay out of the direct line of sight of the approaching hogs. What I mean is that you should be sure that you do not put any decoys directly in front of you as you hunt hogs. If the wind is at your back and the decoy is in front of you, the hog is likely going to approach the decoy from the opposite side of the decoy meaning that they will be walking directly towards you to get to the decoy.

So as you set up your decoys, you should keep this in mind because if the hog is looking in your direction the entire time they approach the decoy, there is a much higher chance that they will spot you compared to when you are sitting off to the side. Try placing the decoy out in front of you but at more of an angle so that you are off to the side as the hog makes its approach.

Avoid Body Silhouette

Another tip to stay concealed from the sight of hogs is to avoid a body silhouette. This goes along with having your back to the sun which I described earlier but what I am talking about is if you are standing or sitting in a location where there is nothing behind you then there is a much higher chance that a hog can see you compared to when you have something behind you to cover the outline of your body. Take the above picture for an example. It is pretty easy to see the person standing on the top of the image because they are standing on the highest elevation of the hill.

In contrast, the person standing below them would be much more difficult to see them as they would have ground behind them to help cover their silhouette. So the quick and simple tip about this is to always make sure that there is something behind you so you do not stick out like a sore thumb. You could sit in front of rocks, trees, bushes, fences or pretty much anything else that is at least as big as you are so there is something blocking out your body outline. When walking along hills try not to walk at the tallest peaks as again your silhouette can be seen like the above example. Instead, walk down the hillside about 20 yards lower than the peak elevation of the hills so that there is always ground behind you if a hog is looking at the hill from down below or from a hillside adjacent to the one you are on.

Camouflage & Face Paint

Hogs do have decent vision so you really need to ensure that your clothing is blended well with your surroundings. Make sure that you select a camouflage pattern that mixes well with the type of area you are going to hunt. There are ton of different camouflage patterns on the market and each has its own purpose. Some of the patterns match better with trees while other patterns mix better with grass and vegetation. Just be aware of these differences as you purchase your hunting clothing. Also, if you will be hunting in the winter it can be a good idea to buy white winter camouflage as this will help conceal you best in the snow.

In addition to camouflage it can be a good idea to put on face paint. Exposed skin can really stick out to the vision of hogs, so just a little bit of face paint can go a long way in staying concealed. The good news is camo face paint is inexpensive and easy to apply so implementing its use into your hunting strategy should not take a whole lot of effort or cost.

Scent Control

One of the strongest defense mechanisms that hogs have is their sense of smell. They can smell human scent from incredible distances. If they catch the slightest whiff of something unfamiliar they will run away in a hurry. In order to get rid of as much human scent as possible you will want to take as many precautions as possible to control the amount of scent you give off. It is pretty much impossible to eliminate 100% of the scent that will be on you and your equipment, but implementing these tips should greatly reduce the chances of being scented by the hog.

Ways to control scent:

- Hang hunting clothes outside for several days in advance of the hunt

- Wash your clothes in scent-control soap from a sporting goods store

- Use scent-killing soap when you take a shower

- Buy scent-blocking hunting clothes

- Use scent-blocking spray all over your clothes prior to heading into the field

Hang hunting clothes outside for several days in advance of the hunt

One of the easiest of the above recommendations is airing out your hunting clothes in advance. This should be everything including your coat, pants, boots, gloves etc. What you should do is hang your clothes outside for at least 3-4 days in advance of your hunt to have the outside air eliminate any smell. The time in the outdoors allows most of the human smells to get covered up with the natural outside smells.

Wash your clothes in scent-control soap

Never wash your hunting clothes with regular laundry detergent. Pretty much every kind of regular laundry detergent has some type of fragrance which will absolutely be a detriment to your hunting experience. Either do not use soap at all or buy special soap sold at hunting stores specifically designed for hunting that does not have odor.

Use scent-killing soap when you take a shower

In addition to not washing your clothes with regular laundry detergent with fragrances, you also do not want to use regular soap when you take a shower prior to hog hunting. Again, pretty much every kind of shower soap will have some fragrances included and that is something you do not want. At sporting goods stores they sell soaps that are designed for hunting and they do not have any fragrances included. Additionally, you should not put on regular deodorant. Again, you can get non-fragranced deodorant at a sporting goods store.

Buy scent-blocking hunting clothes

Another thing you can consider in attempting to block as much scent from the hogs as possible is to buy scent-blocking hunting clothes. There are several brands that produce camouflage clothing that claim to have scent-blocking built into the fabric. Now if you are just getting into the sport and have a limited budget you should not let this hinder you from hunting as you should use what you have access to for starting. However, after time when you are ready to upgrade your hunting clothes you can consider this. I will say that this is not a 100% necessary thing to do because you can use the other tips to reduce the scent from your clothing, but if your budget allows, the scent-blocking camouflage is a good option.

Use scent-blocking spray all over your clothes prior to heading into the field

Finally you can purchase a scent blocking spray for your clothes. Essentially this scent-blocking spray comes in a spray bottle and you can apply this to your clothing just before hunting. Simply spray the scent blocker all over you clothes prior to walking out to your hunting spot. This can be a good final way to reduce your scent. The sprays are usually affordable and you can get a bottle for about $5-$10 that should last you for multiple hunting trips.

Now let's discuss using decoys to fool hogs...

Step 14: Decoying

Use Decoys to Add Realism to Your Setup

Decoys can be a great tool for attracting hogs, although decoying hogs is much less common compared to other types of game animals. In most cases you will be calling for hogs which I will discuss later, but it is important to note that using a decoy of some sort along with calling can work in bagging hogs. This is because as a hog approaches the location where they hear the calling sounds coming from, they are looking to validate the item that is making the sound.

Make sure that you place any decoys in a location that is highly visible to the approaching hogs. You should try to place them on higher spots in the field such as ridges, mounds or clearings in the field where the decoy can be easily seen from any direction. This is critical as you want the hog to see the decoy as they come toward the sound of the call.

Place Decoys Out of Direct Line of Sight

Another tip to try when you use decoys is to place the decoy out of the direct line of sight of you as the hunter. Since hogs may approach the bait from downwind so they can smell the bait as they approach, if you are hunting from upwind it would put you directly in the sight line of the hog. Just be aware of this and try to avoid it.

DECOY PLACEMENT

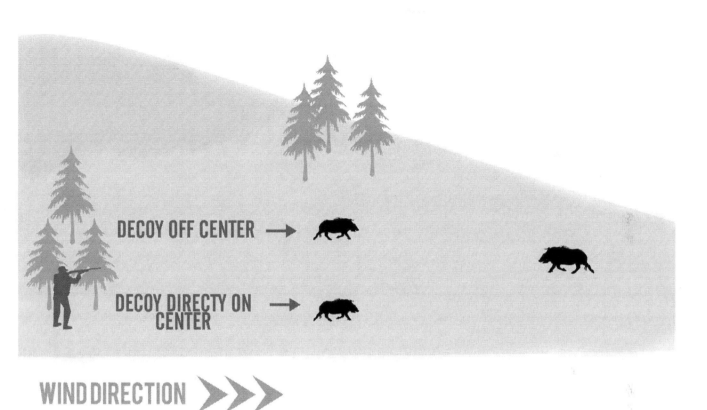

The above is an example of placing your decoys slightly off center from the hunter. As you can see the decoy on the bottom of the image is in the direct line of sight with the hunter. As the hog would approach the decoy from right to left he would be looking directly at the location where the hunter is. In contrast, the decoy above this is slightly off center. Simply placing the decoy 20-40 yards off the center will help pull the eyes of the approaching hog away from the hunter. The hunter will still be in excellent shooting range as the hog approaches.

Now let's take a look at calling for hogs…

Step 15: Call Types and Sounds

Hog Calls to Grab Attention

Communicating with hogs by calling for them can be a very satisfying and unique experience. With some practice you can become effective at drawing hogs close enough for shooting which will greatly improve your success. Let's take a look at the advantages of each of these call types.

Types of Hog Calls

- Mouth Calls

- Electronic Calls

Mouth Calls

Mouth calls are one of the staples to hog hunting and have been around for many years in the hog hunting world. Basically, they are a plastic or wooden calls that you hold with your hands and you blow through them to imitate the sounds of hogs. Depending on how you blow them, they can make a wide range of sounds like distress sounds. One consideration with mouth calls is that they can take a little time to get used to. It can also take time to learn how to call them in a manner that accurately recreates a hog sound. However, once you get the calling down, they can be very realistic in sound and you may find it personally satisfying to call hogs with a mouth call versus an electronic call. Mouth and hand hog calls are usually some of the least expensive call types, typically starting around $15.

Another advantage of mouth calls is their small size and ease of transport. Most mouth calls are around 4-8 inches long so they are extremely convenient to carry around. Simply throw them in your coat pocket and you are all set to go. In contrast, electronic callers are much larger, including the calling unit itself along with the remote control. This adds a fair amount of extra equipment which can be a nuisance especially when you are making long walks to your hunting spot or when you are moving spots often. There is also no setup time for mouth calls where electronic calls can take about 10-15 minutes to get set up. Also, when you are setting up an electronic call in the field you are exposed to the sight of nearby hogs the entire time you are setting up.

Hopefully you take the opportunity to try mouth calling at some point and see how it works for you and the areas you hunt. As I mentioned there are many benefits to using mouth calls but the one consideration is learning how to call with mouth calls effectively. Keep in mind entire books have been written on this topic. To learn more about how to use a mouth call I would recommend looking into some of the following resources.

Resources to learn how to mouth call for hogs:
- Owner's manual included with call (many come with some basic tips)
- CDs sold at hunting stores
- YouTube videos (simply search for hog calling videos)
- Online hunting forums
- Fellow hunters

Electronic Calls

Electronic calls have made a huge insurgence into hog hunting over the last few decades due to their effectiveness and ease of use. Basically an electronic call is a speaker system that you can place out in the field and then with most models you can use a remote control to turn the unit on and make sounds that hogs are attracted to. Electronic hog calls range in cost from about $40 to $400 or more but are very much worth the investment due to the increased hunting success.

The nice thing about electronic calls is that most models have a huge variety of sounds they can reproduce. In contrast, with a mouth call you are typically constrained to just one type of animal per call. This means that if you test one animal call and you are not getting results, you will need to use an entirely different call to produce the sounds of another animal. However, with electronic calls you simply push a different button and you can get the sound of a completely different animal.

You can potentially save some money with electronic calls because most models have the capability for multiple sounds. Some calling systems even have the ability to add different sound packages in the future that you can upgrade to. Here are some sounds that electronic calls can make.

Electronic call sounds:

- Hogs in Distress

- Feeding Hogs

- Grunts

- Snorts

- Piglets

- Aggressive Hogs

- And more…

Another advantage of electronic calls is that there is really no learning curve as there is with mouth calls. With an electronic call all you need to do is simply push the button on the remote and you can turn on the call with extremely lifelike sound. Not only is the sound extremely lifelike but you can vary the sound and volume with just a few pushes of the button and really no training or practice at all. This ease of use makes electronic calls a great option for beginning hog hunters.

Additionally, electronic calls free up your hands for shooting. Simply push the button on the electronic call and let the machine do the work for you as you wait for the hogs to come within shooting distance. Once they are close enough, there will be no need to put down a mouth call as your hands are free and ready to take aim and fire.

Call Sounds and Timing

When calling for hogs it is important to know that there is wide range of sounds that can bring hogs to your hunting location. Additionally, each type of call sound has its own purpose to create a specific response from the nearby hogs. For example, a hog distress call indicates that there is a wounded or threatened hog in the area, so a sow hog may come to the sound to see what is going on. In contrast, a feeding frenzy call would indicate to hogs that other hogs are feeding so they would come to the area to feed.

Sample Types of hog calls:

- **Aggressive Hog**- Hogs, particularly boars can be territorial animals so if you use a challenge aggressive call this could entice them to the area. They do not want other hogs in their area so using challenge calls can be effective to pull in a few boars that are ready to drive that intruder out.
- **Hog Distress**- Using this type of call can be effective in tricking other hogs into thinking one of their piglets are in danger, which can be particularly effective after sows have recently have given birth to their young. The sows may come running to see what is going on and make sure their piglets are okay. In addition, it can bring in random hogs from sheer curiosity.
- **Feeding**- Another effective call is a feeding call which is essentially a call of hogs that are currently feeding. This is great when you are hunting over a baiting area as the nearby hogs are likely to be interested in a easy meal.

I do want to point out that this is a list of some of your most common hog call sounds along with the basic purpose that each one serves in successful hog hunting. Please be aware that there is wide range of variations to each of these as well as many other calls that can be effective as you expand your hog hunting skills. As a beginning to intermediate hog hunter, I would recommend that you start with these call types as you work to get experience and success.

After you start mastering some of these calls, then it is great to add some additional sounds to your hog calling vocabulary. However, it is best to not complicate things too much as you get into the sport and become frustrated. There is a ton to learn with hog hunting so build your skills and expand from there. Think of it like riding a bike. When you first learn it is about the basics of balancing, starting and stopping. You do not start off riding wheelies and jumping curbs. Those are all fun things to add down the road, but you must first start with a good foundation before expanding into more advanced tactics.

Calling Frequency

Another consideration with calling hogs is the calling frequency as you work hogs into your hunting area. What I mean by calling frequency is how often you call for hogs. You actually have several options with this. You could elect to continually call for hogs until you get one to come in shooting range, or you may only call a few times in hopes of pulling in hogs. What is the perfect amount of calling? Well this is really where experience and trial and error comes into play. Some people leave an electronic caller on the entire time they hunt and never turn it off. Other hunters prefer to cycle the call on and off.

People have had plenty of success with both methods and it is really up to you to try out and see what works best for you and your area or even the specific hogs you have near you for that hunt. For example, if you have a very active hogs responding to you with every call you make, then it might be good to just keep calling. However, you may have times where the calls are more intermittent and it can work to cycle your calling and give a few minutes in between calls. Again, there is really no perfect answer to the amount of calling because people have had success with all frequencies and each individual hog may react differently.

What If You Don't Get Any Response?

There will be some times when you call for hogs and do not get a response. Hopefully you have used the tips about scouting your hunting area in advance to do your best to confirm that there are hogs around. However, there will be times when the hogs have moved out or are just not cooperating that day. It is important to give each hunting spot a good 20-30 minutes of calling to see if you get a response. There will be times that it takes much longer for hogs to react or come within range to be able to hear your calls, but about 20-30 minutes can be an appropriate amount of time to start with.

If possible, try to have at least 2-3 hunting spots scouted out and ready to hunt. It is going to take more time and effort to have a few spots lined up, but this will give you some great flexibility on the times you do get out hunting. If you set up at one of your hunting locations and call for 30 minutes without response, you can then pack up and head to the next location. Even if you are having success it can be nice to have a few spots lined up. Let's say you go to location 1 and shoot 3 hogs in 20 minutes. That is a great success but you have now likely killed the nearby hogs and scared the rest away. Having a second spot lined up will allow you to keep your hunt going.

Now let's talk about hunting in the daylight...

Step 16: Day Hunting

Use Hog Behavior to Your Benefit

The good news is that hogs can be hunted at pretty much any time of day, but each time does have its challenges and opportunities. I encourage you to try hog hunting during all times of the day and see what works best for you and your area. In this section I will discuss daylight hunting and how it can be productive for hog hunting.

Considerations for Day Hunting:

- Morning

- Afternoon

- Sunset

- Location

- Shooting distance

- Stalking hogs

- Calling

- Silhouette effect

- Scanning for hogs

Mornings

Taking advantage of the morning feeding time is an excellent way to bag some hogs. As the sun is getting ready to come up in the morning and for the first few hours of the morning the hogs are quite active. A majority of other animals begin to get off their resting spots and get active as they prepare for their first meal of the day. For you as the hunter you now have the advantage of shooting hogs when they pursue their first meal of the day.

If you are hunting for hogs first thing in the morning the chances are that you will get some excellent hunting opportunities. Check the areas that have plenty of vegetation or areas where you have baited. You should also check near any bodies of water or standing water in your area. For example, maybe there is a pond or swampy area on the property you are hunting. Since this would be a great source of water for the hogs and their food sources, you are likely to find some hanging out nearby.

Afternoon

It is possible to have hog hunting success during the entire day. If you only have a small amount of time to go hog hunting and it happens to be in the afternoon you can still be successful. The afternoons have better visibility due to the sun being higher in the sky. The warmer temperatures in the afternoon can also be a benefit for your comfort as a hunter.

However, the afternoon is likely going to be the slowest time for hunting hogs as they will often rest during this time because they do not like the high heat. Since they are not as active during this time it is less likely that you will see hogs. Although when hogs are very hungry and are having a tough time finding food you could lure them out in the afternoon.

Additionally it can help to try different hunting times to mix things up. Let's say you and other hunters in your area always hunt at the peak hunting times of early morning and around sunset. The hogs may become accustomed to these patterns and get leery of hunting for their prey during those times. This means that you could benefit from hunting at a different than usual time to trick some of those skittish older hogs.

One of the best areas to find hogs in the warm afternoons is near water sources or near muddy areas. They will often be using these muddy pits and water to cool off so if you know where these areas are the chances of finding hogs nearby is pretty likely.

Sunset

Similar to the morning, hogs come out at sunset to feed. Again, hogs will be feeding at this time of day so it means that the hogs are going to be active in trying to take advantage of that daylight in hopes of finding their own food or going to feeding bait piles. In the opinion of many hog hunters the last half hour of sunlight to 1 hour after sunset is one of the absolute best times to find hogs out and in a good spot to be able to shoot. If you are going to hunt into the late afternoon and early evening I would recommend that you bring a flashlight with you. This way if you end up being far out in the woods as it gets dark, you will have a light to help you find your way back.

Location

It is always important to make your hunting location choice wisely when you are hunting hogs but you may be wondering what makes a good hunting location during the day. Well hopefully the scouting that you have done has helped you locate a spot where you have reason to believe there should be some hogs in the area.

A great place to start with hunting locations for daytime is near trails that come out of woods and into an open area. Hogs will often follow the natural trails in the woods that deer and other animals have created. This makes hunting near these trails an excellent choice to start your hunt because as you call for hogs it is likely that they will approach the open area from one of these trails in the woods.

During the daytime you can also try to get to high elevation points to improve your sight distance. This is an advantage that daytime hunting has over nighttime hunting. Look for any natural hills, ridgelines and any other higher points in the area that you could use to get elevated. By being high up in the air you are going to be able to greatly increase the distance you can see the hogs. Of course when you are at higher spots it can put you in a position where you might be more susceptible to being seen by hogs, so ensure that you find plenty of covering as you sit in these higher spots. Also pay attention to how you can best get to this high spot without being heavily exposed to the sight of hogs as you travel to the spot.

Shooting Distance

One advantage to daytime hunting compared to evening hunting is the greater visibility you will have. Sure, in the evening you can use spotlights to see in the dark but even with spotlights your sight distance will be limited compared to long sight distances you have during the day. Especially if you utilize binoculars and scopes for rifles you can see several hundred yards or more during the daylight hours. In addition, during the evening you can use methods like stalking hogs to get even closer. This technique is challenging in the evening as you cannot see hogs from long distances.

Stalking Hogs

Hopefully, through calling, baiting and the other techniques you learn in this book you will be able to pull in the hogs for close shots, but there are times where the hogs will be out in a distance and you will need to stalk them to be able to get within shooting range. For example, let's say you are hunting an area that has a lot of hills and changes in elevation. It is possible that you will spot a hog that is out in the distance but too far away to shoot. In this case it can work well to stalk your hog to bring yourself in close enough shooting distance. Let's take a look at an example of this technique in action.

STALKING

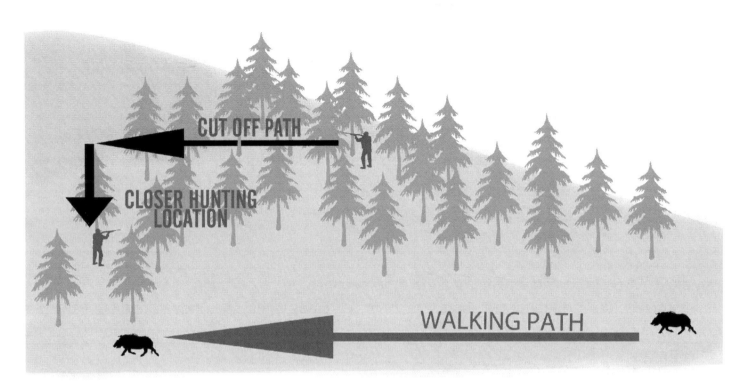

In this example, the hunter is initially towards the top of a hill in the middle of the picture. Then the hunter spots a hog towards the bottom of the hill but the distance is too far to be able to shoot the hog from his current location. This is a great time where you can use the stalking technique to close the gap and make better shooting opportunities. The first thing to do is identify what direction the hog is walking in. In this case the hog's walking path is from right to left on the image. Based on this path the hunter is going to try to get out in front of the hog's walking path on the left and cut him off.

The hunter's first move is to stay high on the hill and walk a good distance to the left so that he can get far enough out in front of the hog's walking path before he closes in for a better shot. He wants to stay high on the hill and behind as much cover as possible to avoid being spotted by the hog. After the hunter has made it far enough ahead of the hog's walking path he is going to drop elevation a little bit and walk partially down the hill into his new hunting spot. Remember you still have the wind to deal with so do not get directly in front of the hog because in this case the wind is blowing left to right so it will blow your odor towards the hog. However, if you remain high enough above the hog's walking path you can still be in good position to shoot.

Now that the hunter has made it to this advanced position he can wait for the hog to continue along its walking path. As you can see when the hog keeps walking from right to left he is eventually going to be directly below the position where the hunter is. When the hog reaches this point the hunter will be in a much closer shooting position compared to the initial spot where he started.

Silhouette Effect

Another tip to remember during this time of day is the silhouette effect. I discussed this in step 12 with wind and sun direction tips but I want to bring it up here again as a reminder. When you are walking around during the day you will be much more susceptible to being seen by hogs compared to the evening hours when you can use the lack of light to get to your hunting spot more easily without being seen.

Remember that when you are walking during the day you want to try to avoid being out in wide open spaces because the hogs can see you more clearly. Particularly if you are walking in an area with the wind at your back the hogs will be able to see your outline from a long distance away. Always critically examine where your hunting spot is and plan the best way to walk there without being exposed. Sometimes that means that you will have to walk significantly farther as well as go through challenging terrain, but if you do not factor this in, the hogs will bust you. If you are busted by the hogs you will have no chance of shooting any once you get to your hunting spot.

Now let's identify tips for hunting in the evening...

Step 17: Evening Hunting

Use the Cover of the Night for a Great Hunt

If you are looking for a very exciting hunting experience then night hunting for hogs could be just for you. Since hogs are often active at night and that means that these hunts can be some of the most productive hog hunts you may ever have. Let's take a look at some of the considerations for successful evening hunting.

Considerations for Evening Hunting:

- Location

- Calling

- Lighting

- Scanning for hogs

- Shooting distance

- Retrieving your kill

- Safety

Location

Choosing your location for hunting in the evening is an important consideration for successfully bagging hogs. Because your sight will be hindered by the minimal amount of light you will want to make sure that you are positioned in a clear and open area for best hog spotting possibilities. Evening hunts in thick woods are going to be more challenging due to the lack of light so an easier spot to set up would be alongside an open field or prairie and near baiting areas.

Although the dark does hinder your ability to see the hogs it also provides a benefit to you because you are able to use the natural concealment of the dark to keep hidden from the hogs. This does not mean that you can be loud or move around more than you can during the daylight hours, but you will have some advantages. For example, in the daylight you need to be very aware of the silhouette effect which is essentially making sure that your body is not out in the open. This is because with the sun to your back the hogs can spot the outline of a human quite easily. In the evening you can actually stand on the side of a field and not worry about the silhouette effect and get yourself in a good position for shooting hogs out in the open.

Lighting

One critical component and difference between daytime hunting and evening hunting is the use of artificial lighting with your hunt. However, before you start using lighting for hog hunting it is important to check your local regulations and see if they have any rules against the use of lighting or the type of lighting that you can use.

There are few lighting methods that you can consider when hunting in the dark. One option is to use the spotlight method. A spotlight can either be mounted to a vehicle or a high candle power handheld unit. Either way is fine. It is just important that you have a very bright spotlight to shine further out into the dark as well as to illuminate any hogs you do find so that when it becomes time to shoot you will be able to easily see your target. One downside of using a handheld unit is that if you are hunting alone it will be challenging to keep the spotlight on the hog as you prepare to shoot.

Another popular option is to have a gun-mounted light. These are particularly common and useful when using a rifle. Many hog rifles will have the ability to add one of these lights as an attachment and they are extremely handy because wherever you point your rifle it will be illuminating that exact spot to locate hogs. When you do locate a hog you will be in a good position to take a quick shot since your rifle is already aimed in that direction.

Finally, you could also consider a headlamp. The benefit of these is that whatever way you turn your head, the light from the headlamp will follow. In addition, you benefit because unlike a handheld spotlight your hands are freed up so you are able to use your hands the entire time to hold and aim your gun. Headlamps are probably a better option when hunting with a shotgun as you will be at closer ranges as not all of the headlamps have as much power as some of the handheld units.

All of these lighting methods are effective. It is just important for you evaluate what is best for you and the hunting situation. Ask yourself what distances you plan to hunt from and the weapon style you want to use. Also consider if you are going to be hunting with a partner or not. When hunting solo you will likely want to use a gun-mounted light or a headlamp so your hands are free to hold your gun.

Scanning for Hogs

Before we get completely off the subject of lighting, let's talk a little more about the specific strategy to use with lighting. There are two things in particular to help identify hogs when hunting in the dark. The first is the shine of their eyes. Chances are that even if you have never been hog hunting before you have at least seen the eyes of animals such as cats or dogs in the dark and have seen the glow or shine that they give off when light hits them. This is the exact same thing that you will notice with hogs as well.

In order to see their eyes, the best thing to do is use a scanning method with your lights where you start with shining your lights off to the far left side of the area you are hunting and work the light back to the right side. I recommend doing this often to locate any hogs. You can also do this by scanning back and forth at different distances. What I mean is that your first scan from left to right can be at a range that is closer to you, let's just say 50-75 yards or so. Then when you scan back from right to left scan at 75-150 yards and then on your final scan from left to right go to the furthest your light can reach of maybe around 200 yards.

After you complete this scan you should start back over from the closest distance to the furthest distance. Keep doing this continually until you spot the eyes of hogs. Also with this technique you can share the responsibility with your hunting buddy. You can take one half of the area to scan and your partner can take the other half. Switching what side of the area you scan with your partner can be effective as well. This is because after you look at an area for some time you may miss something so having a fresh set of eyes may help you pick out more hogs than if you never switched sides.

One more way that is effective in locating hogs is the silhouette method. What I mean here is that sometimes there may be lights out in the distance that you can use to assist if you see anything walk in between you and the light. For example, there might be a yard light from a nearby farm that you can see in the distance. You can try lining yourself up with that yard light and an open path in the field that is likely for a hog to walk past. If a hog walks on that path you will see a flash of black move across the path and then you will know that something is nearby.

Shooting Distance

One more consideration and factor with hunting in the evening is the difference in shooting distances you can take compared to hunting in the daylight hours. When hunting during the day your shooting distance will only be limited by the effective range of your weapon and your ability to see far distances. Of course your sight distance can be increased with the use of optics.

In the evening your range is going to be much more limited because you can only see as far as the light you are using. Even with a spotlight it is not always feasible to take accurate shots at several hundred yards in the dark. It is best to plan for shots with a rifle of about 100-200 yards at the max to ensure that you will be able to see the hogs well. There are people who have had luck with further distances but just be aware of this range recommendation so that you can plan to set up in a place where your shots do not need to be hundreds of yards.

When you plan out your location well you can hopefully get the hogs to be much closer than 200 yards and those shots in the dark will be more manageable. Implementing decoys and effective calling strategies should allow you to have shorter range shots so you do not have to push the limits of sight to shoot hogs at night.

Retrieving Your Kill

When hunting at night it is important to remember that with the limited light is likely to make it more challenging to find your hog after you shoot it. As simple as it may seem, it can actually be quite difficult to find the exact spot that you shot the hog after you make your shot and walk out to the kill spot. There is an entire section of this book coming up where I discuss retrieving your kill but I want to cover a few specific tips here regarding retrieving your hog in the dark.

The first thing that will make retrieving your kill easier to do in the dark is to keep an eye on the hog after you shoot it. Sometimes when you shoot a hog it is not going to fall over dead instantly and may run a little bit away. Try to follow the hog as far as you can if it does run after being shot.

Then after the hog has stopped moving or once it reaches a point where you can no longer see, it is important to make a mental note of this spot. You can use a physical marker in the field to help you in locating the hog. For example, there might be a tree near the area you last saw the hog or there might be a little change in elevation in that spot. Whatever you can use as a physical marker it is fine because as you walk out to retrieve the hog you can use this marker to guide you to a close enough spot where you can begin your search.

Safety

Although I already had a previous section completely dedicated to safety it is important to bring up safety again for night hunting as hunting in the dark does create more safety challenges. The obvious challenge is that hunting in the dark greatly hinders the ability for you to see long distances and see anything that may be around the direction you are shooting. Even with the use of spotlights your vision can still be somewhat hindered and seeing well beyond where you are pointing your spotlight is really not possible.

You really need to ensure that you communicate well with your hunting partner for evening hunting. If you plan on standing right next to each other as you hunt in the evening that is one thing and it should be much easier to know where each other are located. However, there are probably going to be times where you will split up in order to cover more ground in hopes of improving your chances of success.

When you do hunt with a partner you should know the land well that you are hunting or look at a map together in depth before going out. Discuss where each person is going to hunt from and clearly identify together the safe shooting angles that you have. You should also discuss how each person is going to walk to and from their hunting location. Finally, be sure that you communicate with each other during the hunt if something changes your plan. For example, one of you might wound a hog that you need to track. If this tracking is going to bring you off your planned hunting spots make sure you call your partner and inform them of your change of plans.

Hunting with a buddy can add to the fun and success of your hunt...

Step 18: The Buddy System

Use a Buddy to Improve Success

Hunting for hogs can be a great way to enjoy the outdoors by yourself but it can also be a fun way to spend some time with friends or family. Not only is it fun to share the experience but hunting with a partner can also help improve your success rate.

Benefits of hunting with a partner:

- Extra set of eyes
- Calling
- Two guns
- Be safe

Extra Set of Eyes

Hogs can be challenging to spot, especially in areas covered with a lot of natural vegetation such as trees, brush and tall grass. They are also challenging to pick out when you are trying to spot them from long distances. This makes it beneficial to have a buddy with as you can both be on the lookout for approaching hogs. One of you may see a hog that the other hunting partner missed.

Try sitting next to each other or even back to back. This way you can each focus on covering a certain area. You can essentially double the area that you can scout by adding a buddy. However, it can also be useful to trade off areas that you are looking at. What I mean is that after 10 or 15 minutes if you do not see hogs you could alternate the spots you are watching. This can be effective because after looking at one area for a long time you may miss something where switching things up and having a fresh pair of eyes look over the area could help spot the cunning hogs.

Calling

One huge benefit to hunting with a buddy is calling for the hogs. This is particularly true when using a mouth call or hand call but it can also be beneficial when using electronic calls. When you are hunting by yourself it will be up to you to do all of the calling for the hogs so if you are doing this with a mouth call your hands will be tied up using the call rather than holding your weapon in preparation for the hog to get within shooting range. Even if you are using an electronic call you will need to use your hands some to operate the remote controls.

When you bring a buddy with you can share this responsibility and tag team hogs. For example, your buddy could do the mouth calling and this will allow you to focus completely on any approaching hogs. The buddy can also operate the remote controls of the electronic calls. You may not always want to leave the calls running all of the time because it can actually be effective to turn them on and off intermittently to peak the interest of nearby hogs, so your partner can do this for you. After you have bagged a hog or two you can switch responsibilities and give your buddy the chance to shoot the next hog.

BUDDY HUNTING

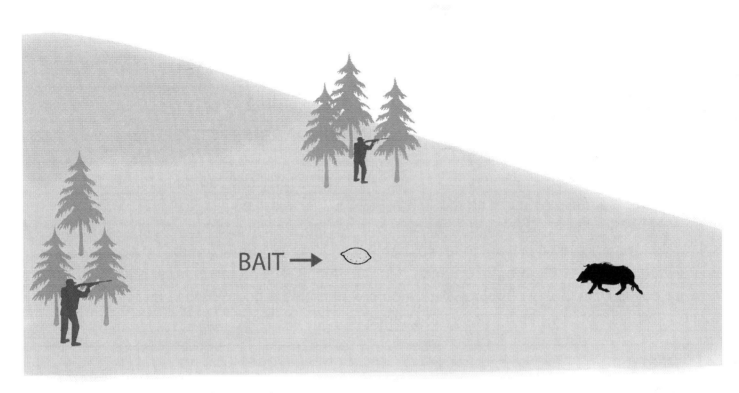

WIND DIRECTION ▶▶▶

Another benefit when hunting with a buddy is that you can hunt from different locations and have one of the hunters call for the hog while the other hunter is the shooter. A good strategy to try is having the hunter who is to the far upwind side, in this example the left side, be the one who does the calling for the hog. Then the hunter who is towards the top of the image be the shooter. This shooter would be somewhat downwind but off to the side of the bait. As the hogs approach the bait this shooter should have good shooting opportunities. After the shooter has a chance to bag a hog or two, you can change roles and let the other person be the shooter.

Two Guns

Another benefit of having your buddy with for your hog hunting trip is that you will now have two guns rather than one. Particularly if you are using bait and you are comfortable with leaving them on or operating the remotes while handling your weapons, you both can have guns ready to shoot.

With two guns one hunter may miss their shot at the hog and the other hunter could be prepared to follow up with a quick second shot at the hog before it runs out of shooting range. In addition, this technique could be beneficial when more than one hog is approaching your hunting spot. The two of you could time out your shots and shoot at the same time as best as possible. This way you could end up with two hogs down rather than just one had you been hunting alone.

Be Safe

Anytime you are using weapons it is very important to keep safety in mind. You never want to have a fun hunting situation turn into an unfortunate event and have someone get hurt. This aspect is increased when you are hunting with a buddy compared to hunting by yourself because you want to make sure that you never fire your weapon in the direction that your buddy is located.

It is important to always tell each other where you are going to be hunting from and plan out your hunting locations in advance and communicate this well with each other. Even when you have discussed hunting spots with your buddy you should still be cautious when you are preparing to take a shot. Something may have happened that caused your partner to move from their planned hunting spot so be sure that you scan around the area that you are shooting at to ensure nobody is in that vicinity. If you are ever unsure if you are taking a safe shot, do not shoot. It is better to miss out on a shot at a hog over injuring a friend.

Now let's identify effective shooting techniques…

Step 19: Deadly Shot Placement

Successfully Bag Your Hog

When you finally have a hog within effective shooting range it is one of those moments that makes your heart race. This moment can be brief so you need to quickly take action to bag the hog. You must always be prepared because hogs are leery and as soon as they notice anything out of ordinary they will quickly run away and be out of effective shooting distance. Use these tips to make the most out of your shooting opportunities.

Shooting tips:

- Practice shooting before the hunting season
- Be patient
- Select a clear shooting lane
- Get the hog to stop
- Shot placement
- Improving shot accuracy
- Learn from missed shots

Practice Shooting Before the Hunting Season

If you have never been hog hunting or if you are having difficulty hitting hogs then it might be a good idea to get in some target practice before your next hunting trip. If you do not have your own land, one of the easiest and most cost effective ways to practice shooting is to visit a firing range. Chances are you live within a half hour of a firing range where you can pay a fee to practice shooting. This is usually inexpensive as you can buy a time slot, usually in hour or half hour increments, for less than $20. This minimal investment could greatly improve your success on your next hunting trip.

However, it is not always necessary to go to a firing range. If you own your own land you could certainly use that to practice shooting or if the land that you are going to be doing your hog hunting on is available for target practice you could use that as well. The one thing to keep in mind is if you do plan on target practicing on the same land that you will be hunting on, I would recommend doing it many days or even week in advance. This is because it is likely the shooting may scare away hogs so do this in advance to leave enough time for the hogs to return to the area.

Be Patient

It is so important to be patient when you are hunting for hogs. The temptation to shoot right away when you see a hog is so strong but you must hold back until the hog slows down to a reasonable rate or stops altogether. Unless you are hunting with a shotgun, the chance of hitting a hog that is running is slim, even for the most experienced hunters. In most cases you need to give the hog a chance to stop for the best possible chance to hit it.

Sometimes the hogs head directly to the bait and get quickly within shooting range. However, many times they run around for a while as they investigate what is going on. They are simply checking out the sounds and what they see before heading directly towards their food.

Again, as tempting as it might be to shoot right away, it is so critical to be patient and hold tight until you have a higher-percentage shot. If not, you will end up wasting a lot of ammunition and scaring off many hogs that you could have eventually had a better shot at if you waited a little longer for them to stop moving and get into closer shooting range.

Select a Clear Shooting Lane

Waiting for a clear shooting lane goes hand in hand with being patient. You want to try to get into a position where you can see the hog and not have a lot of grass, hills, rocks or anything blocking the way of your shot. This is easy to say but in reality it is difficult, especially if you are hunting in the summer when the fields are likely to be covered with tall vegetation. This is where some skill and practice come into play.

Some times you can only see part of the hog. The hog may just have its head sticking around the back side of a rock or the hog might have half of its body covered by tall grass. Now is when you need to decide whether or not to take the shot. If you have a shot at the hog, regardless of how small of a portion of the hog it might be, you need to decide if this is going to be your best opportunity to shoot this hog.

If you think that this is your best chance then go ahead and take the shot. However, if you feel that you may get a better shot if you wait then go ahead and wait. Shooting and missing is likely going to cause the hog to run away and you may not get any other chances to shoot this hog. Also, a shot may scare off any other hogs in the area as well so it is just important to make your best educated guess if you should wait. If you miss it does not mean that you cannot call back in that hog because sometimes you will be able to call it back, but just as many times it will scare off the hog and it will never be seen again on that hunting trip.

Get the Hog to Stop

Another thing that you can do when the hogs are out in the open is to make a sound to get them to stop. You can simply make a noise such as a dog bark or whistle sound to grab their attention. This will be effective in getting them to stop briefly to see what made the sound. You only want to do this if you are ready to take a quick shot because if you wait to shoot, the noise is likely going to scare them away after they have stopped for a moment to examine the sound.

Shot Placement

Now that a hog is in shooting range let's discuss where you should attempt to place your shot. The two primary shot locations you want to focus on when shooting hogs are the head and the heart/lung areas. Both of these have some advantages and downsides so let's examine each option.

Head

An accurately placed shot at the head, particularly behind the ear, of a hog will provide a very quick and lethal kill. This is because the hog will die pretty much instantly from a well-placed head shot. It will make for a humane kill. Another benefit of headshots is that if you are planning to eat the meat, this will be the best shot for preserving meat. With a shot at the heart or lungs area it is possible to do a fair amount of damage to the meat, especially if your shot is slightly off and hits the front quarters of the legs where a lot of meat is located.

Another benefit of the headshot is that it eliminates a chase to find the hog. In addition, there are many times where a headshot is the only shot that you have at the animal. What I mean is that as the hog walks around there is likely to be brush, grass or trees in the way a good majority of the time. When the hog finally stops there is a chance that some of the body will be covered up and the only shot placement option you have is the head.

However, a headshot can be difficult because hogs are not huge animals and some of them are smaller than others. If you are a less experienced shooter, this might not be the best option for you as it will take a good amount of accuracy to make a shot on a smaller portion of the hog. Also, the further away the hog is, the harder it will be to hit the smaller area of the head compared to its body.

Heart/Lungs

Another effective area to try to shoot the hog is going to be in the heart/lungs. The heart and lungs are located just behind the front legs of the hog about 1/3 of the way up from the bottom of the hogs body. A well-placed shot in this area will also kill the hog pretty quickly and should not result in much of a challenge in finding the hog after shooting it because it will not be able to run far.

The biggest downside of a shot placed in the heart and lungs is the amount of damage that it can cause to the meat hog. For those of you who will be hunting hogs to eat the meat you may want to stay away from body shots. However, for those of you only looking to help thin out a nuisance population of hogs, the body shot can work well for you.

Improving Shot Accuracy

One of the best ways to drastically improve your shooting accuracy is to have a stable surface to rest against when you shoot. I discussed a shooting stick earlier and highly recommend it because they help to keep your gun from swaying back and forth which will create inaccurate shots. It is surprising how difficult it is to stand still and aim effectively without bracing yourself.

How to take better shots:

- Use a shooting stick
- Lean against the side of a tree
- Kneel down and rest your elbow on your knee
- Take a deep breath just before you shoot

All of the above methods are excellent ways to take more accurate shots, with my preference being the utilization of a shooting stick, which I previously discussed. However, if you do not own a shooting stick or it is just not practical for you to bring one with you, these other options could be effective for you. If you are hunting in the woods you should not have much difficulty finding a nearby tree to lean against as you shoot. Kneeling is a good option if there is not another tree nearby that is convenient to lean against. However, in most situations there will be plenty of trees around to use as your stabilizer. Finally, to stabilize your shot you want to take a deep breath just before you shoot. Breathing causes the gun to move up and down. As you get into shooting position and are just about ready to take your shot, take a deep breath. Then aim and slowly let your breath out and pull the trigger. You should find that this technique greatly improves the accuracy of your shots.

Learn From Missed Shots

Any hog hunter has missed shots at hogs. It is important not to get down on yourself when you miss. Hogs are very fast and leery and are not the easiest animal to shoot, so it is okay when you miss shots at hogs. Use missed shots as an opportunity to learn from your mistakes.

Try to evaluate what you did well and what you could have done differently. Did you use something to brace yourself for an accurate shot? Did you allow the hog to get into a clear opening if possible? Did you shoot too soon? These are all questions to ask yourself in order to improve your shooting success. Over time, your hit rates will improve, but keep in mind that it is basically impossible to have 100% accuracy and that is completely okay and normal.

Keep reading to learn how to retrieve the hog you just shot…

Step 20: Retrieving Your Hog

You Hit the Hog, Now What?

After you shoot a hog you will want to retrieve your game. Use these tips to successfully collect your game.

Tips after shooting:

- Wait a few minutes

- Pick out a marker where you shot the hog

- Walk slowly to the hog

- Check to make sure the hog is dead before you grab it

Wait a few minutes

Once you shoot a hog it is normal to be excited and want to head out and collect your harvest right away. However, you should wait about 10-15 minutes before heading out to grab your hog. First you want to make sure that the hog is dead so giving it a few minutes to stop moving can be a good idea. If you head out right away and the hog is still alive it is possible that it will run off and go to a spot where you are unable to retrieve it. However, if you leave it sit for a few minutes it will likely just stay put and die near where it was shot and will be much easier to find.

The other reason to wait a few minutes before heading out is that there is a chance that there is another hog in the area that you can shoot. Sounds of a gun going off may not necessarily scare off all of the nearby hogs so if they had heard your calls or they are heading out to where you had been baiting for days there is still a chance that more hogs will still come out of hiding. If you head out to soon you ruin any chance you would have had at bagging more than one hog at the moment.

Pick out a Marker

As soon as you shoot a hog you want to look for any markings near where the hog was after being shot. Sometimes when you shoot the hog it will drop right in the spot it was shot and should be relatively easy to find. However, there are also times when you shoot a hog that it may run for a bit before falling over dead. Particularly in those cases where the hog moved a bit after being shot it is very important to pay attention to where it stopped and make a mental marker.

For example, pick out a tree, rock or pile of dirt in the area that you can use as a location marker to walk to. This makes it much easier to find your hog. The interesting thing is that when you shoot at something a distance away it is odd how hard it can be to find that spot when you start walking to it. The terrain can just look different and your depth perception can be thrown off. Also, your excitement of shooting a hog can sometimes make you forget exactly where the hog was shot. When you have a marker such as a large rock near where you shot it, you can easily walk to the rock and then locate your hog.

Walk Slowly to the Hog

While you walk to the spot where you think the hog stopped, it is important to proceed slowly. Sometimes you may have just wounded the hog so you want to keep an eye on the ground and any brush or grass and look for movement. On the off chance the hog is still alive and moving it may be necessary to shoot it again.

The other reason you want to walk slowly to the hog is to look for any other hogs in the immediate area. It is not uncommon for more than one hog to be in the same area so there could be others that you could also shoot. Bagging more than one hog at one time is very satisfying.

Following a Blood Trail

In some cases it will be easy to tell that you hit the hog because the hog will have died in the spot that you shot it or there may be a lot of blood. However, there can be times the hog will run a distance before falling over dead.

How can you tell if you hit the hog?

- You find blood
- You find bone fragments
- You find hair

Once you reach the exact spot that you shot the hog and the hog is not there stop and examine the area. If you hit the hog there will likely be some blood, bone fragments or hog hair in the near vicinity. Blood will be the easiest way to track them and it should leave a good trail for you to follow. Once you find the first spots of blood then you will want to survey the area and look for the next spots of blood. Make sure you closely examine the ground for the blood. Many times you can see the shiny blood on leaves, dirt and plants on the ground. In addition, there will be times where the blood is on the side of trees or tall plants that the hog brushed against as they ran away.

Typically you will start to see the direction that the hog went based on the blood trail and you can follow that. Make sure that you stay near the most recent spot of blood and look around for the next drop. Try to not move much until you see the next spot. However, if you must move because you cannot find blood, it is important to mark your last spot that you found blood. You could put a branch in the ground to mark the last spot you found blood. This is extremely important because if you go off looking for blood but do not mark your most recent spot, it will be very difficult to get back on track if you are unsuccessful when looking around.

The technique for tracking blood is basically stay near the last spot of blood you see and visually scan in the direction the blood trail is leading you. However, be aware there can be times where the trail makes quick turns. For example, the hog may have been running straight and all of the sudden made a quick turn. This is why you really need to be aware of the last spot you found blood. When you mark the last blood spot it allows you to carefully scan in a radius and if you do not find blood you can go back to the last blood spot and restart your search from there.

Sometimes blood stops coming out of the hog for a little bit so the trail may stop for 10 yards or so. When you know the last spot, it allows you to make a sweep of the area in a continually larger radius until you find more blood. Additionally, if you are unable to find any more blood you can walk around in the woods and search for the hog and if unsuccessful you can return to the last known blood spot to start the search back over.

Check to Ensure the Hog is Dead Before You Grab It

Before you pick up a hog, it is very important to ensure that the hog is dead. Hogs are very aggressive animals and may charge you if they are not dead. You will first want to stop several feet away and see if you can observe any movement of the hog. I recommend standing there with your gun ready in case you do happen to see movement. Then you are in a position to take a quick shot if necessary. After observing the hog for a few minutes without any movement, then it is time to check if the hog is dead at a closer distance. An easy way to do this is by grabbing a stick that is on the ground and poking the hog to see if it moves. The majority of the time it will be dead but if the hog shows any movement at all you need to quickly finish off the hog.

To do this, take a step or two back and make an accurate shot at the head. A head shot at this close range should kill the hog instantly. Be aware that if you do need to shoot the hog again at a close range, a shot to the body will likely do a fair amount of damage to the meat of the animal so if you were planning to keep the meat you really should try to shoot it in the head. Additionally, you need to be aware of safety with this situation because you do not want to shoot at something close to you and accidentally hit a rock or something and have the bullet ricochet back at you.

Now it's time decide what to do with your hog…

Step 21: Hog Cleaning, Preparation & Preservation

Success! You Shot a Hog, Now What?

Now that you have shot and retrieved your hog it is time to get it ready bring home and prepare for eating. This part of the hog hunting process can actually be a bit of work but it is well worth the effort.

What to do with your hog after bagging it:

- Field Dressing the Hog
- Quartering the Hog
- Transporting the Meat
- Disposing of Unused Parts
- Prepping Meat for Consumption
- Cooking Ideas

Field Dressing the Hog

You should try to clean the hog within 1 hour of shooting it to ensure that the meat is still fresh and does not have a chance to go bad before you get it into a cool area. If you are hunting in cold temperatures you can wait a little longer; however, if it is warm outside you should clean your hog as soon as possible after it was shot.

STEP 1: Lie the hog on its back

STEP 2: Stand by the hind legs of the hog. If there is another hunter with you have them hold the front legs apart. Otherwise, it can be handy to use rope to tie all 4 legs to nearby trees, so the legs are all spread apart. Use your knife to cut the throat of the hog about ½ way down its neck. Be sure to cut through the hide and all of the way through the esophagus.

STEP 3: Use your knife to cut through the hide and breastbone of the hog. This will be the part of the hog that is sticking up the tallest. Try and do this in the exact middle of the breastbone area. Do not cut any deeper than the bone as if you go further you can puncture internal organs which can spoil the meat.

STEP 4: After the breastbone is split, cut through the hide and neck the rest of the way up to where you cut the throat.

STEP 5: Now cut the hide the rest of the way down from the bottom of the breastbone area to the hindquarters. Do this by using one hand to hold the skin/hide as high up as possible away from the stomach area of the hog. Again, be very careful to not puncture the stomach or any of the organs by cutting too deep.

STEP 6: If this is a boar you will want to grab the male organs and cut around both sides of it, so it comes out with the rest of the organs.

STEP 7: Use your knife or bone saw to split the tailbone holding the legs together.

STEP 8: After the tailbone is split reach up and grab the esophagus from the neck area and pull it down towards the bottom of the hog. Along the way keep grabbing and pulling all of the rest of the organs. You should be able to pull pretty much all of the organs out all at the same time.

STEP 9: Once all organs are out of the hog, use your hands and knife to cut off any excess fat or tissue that is sticking to the rib cage hindquarters of the hog.

STEP 10: Lift the hog up from its front legs, if possible, to let any of the excess blood drain out of the body.

STEP 11: If you are doing this at home and have access to buckets of water or a garden hose use them to rinse out the inside cavity of the hog.

Transporting the Meat

With all the entrails cleaned out, it is time to get ready to get the meat packed out. The first thing you will want to do is protect the meat from dirt, dust, and bugs. One of the best ways to do this is to put each quarter inside of a large meat sock or wrap in cheesecloth. A big reason that people complain of "gamey" tasting meat is due to improper care of the meat. If the meat is allowed to get dirty or if bugs get on it there certainly can be an undesired flavor of the meat. So by using meat socks to protect the meat, the flavor should be better preserved. In addition, you will want to ensure that the meat stays at cool temperatures. It is best to keep the meat at 40 degrees or cooler to ensure that the meat stays fresh and does not spoil.

Prepping Meat for Consumption

After you have the hog at your home, you will want to butcher the meat off the bones for eating. Before you start cutting the meat off try your best to trim as much fat off the animal as possible. It is ok to leave some of the smaller bits of fat but for the most part get what you can with a knife. You may also want to consider taking your hog to a butcher to handle this task for you. Sure there is some expense to having the butchering done by a professional but it will also save you a lot of time, and the butcher can cut and wrap your meat into certain cuts. For example, they can wrap your chops and roasts separately making it easy to grab what you need out of the freezer when you are going to make a meal from the hog.

Disposing of Unused Parts

After all of the cleaning has been done you will need to get rid of all of the unused parts. When you field dress your hog, it is typically ok to leave the gut pile of entrails in the field. However, out of curtesy you should pull the gut pile off to the side of main trails that other hunters may be using. The good news is that the guts are typically eaten up quickly by birds and predators in the area within a few days.

Disposing of the bones after removing the meat can be another story. Most city garbage companies will not allow you to put animal bones in the garbage. So before you do that be sure to check with your local garbage company. If it is not allowed a great thing to do is check with local butcher for disposal. They may have a disposal fee and allow you to dispose with them or they are likely to have suggestions of other local places you can get rid of the bones.

Consuming the Meat

Now that you have removed all of the meat from the hog or if you have had the hog processed at a butcher it is time to enjoy your well-earned meat. There are a ton of ways that you can enjoy hog meat. Really, most people will use hog in similar ways to how they use pork from farm raised pigs. Here are just a few examples:

How to Use Hog Meat in Meals:

- Chops
- Grilled Ribs
- Hog Roasts
- Full Hog Roasts
- Ground Meat
- Process into smoked sticks
- Summer sausage
- Jerky

Final Words as You Start Hog Hunting

Congratulations! You have taken your first step in becoming a successful hog hunter.

Success is in Your Hands

Remember that hunting is fun but also challenging. Regardless of the success you have make sure you enjoy the time you spend outdoors.

Just Get Started

Getting started with anything can be challenging at first. Think back to when you first started tying your shoes. At first it was difficult, but after time it became second nature. This can be the same with hog hunting. The more you do it the better you will get.

Make Progress Every Day

Using the steps learned in this book will help improve your hog hunting skills. I encourage you to make some type of progress each day of the season. Keep reading books, follow hunting blogs and watch YouTube videos. Six months from now you will be surprised how far you have come by spending time learning more about hog hunting every day.

95289991R00059

Made in the USA
Columbia, SC
08 May 2018